STEPHE

A Case for Collaborative Governance

STEPHEN HARPER

A Case for Collaborative Governance

Enjoy

Lloyd Mackey

LLOYD MACKEY

ECW PRESS

Published by ECW Press
2120 Queen Street East, Suite 200, Toronto, Ontario, Canada M4E 1E2

LIBRARY AND ARCHIVES CANADA CATALOGUING IN PUBLICATION

Mackey, Lloyd
Stephen Harper : the case for collaborative governance / Lloyd Mackey.

ISBN 10: 1-55022-713-0 (cloth)   ISBN 13: 978-1-55022-713-0
ISBN 10: 1-55022-752-1 (paper)   ISBN 13: 978-1-55022-752-9

1. Harper, Stephen, 1959-   2. Conservative Party of Canada. 3. Canada — Politics
and government — 1993-   4. Christianity and politics — Canada. 5. Conservatism
Canada. 6. Prime ministers — Canada — Biography. 1. Title.

FC636.H37M32 2006   971.07'2092   C2006-904112-1

Cover and Text Design: Tania Craan
Production: Mary Bowness
Cover Photo: Dimitri Soudas
Printing: Marquis

This book is set in Adobe Garamond and Oneloda

With the publication of *Stephen Harper: A Case for Collaborative Governance* ECW Press
acknowledges the generous financial support of the Government of Canada through the
Book Publishing Industry Development Program (BPIDP), the Canada Council for the
Arts, and the Ontario Arts Council, for our publishing activites.

DISTRIBUTION

Canada: Jaguar Book Group, 100 Armstrong Ave., Georgetown, ON L7G 5S4

PRINTED AND BOUND IN CANADA

ECW PRESS
ecwpress.com

CONTENTS

In memory of Chuck Cadman, member of parliament for Surrey North (B.C.), 1997–2005.

Foreword

Lloyd Mackey's book offers many interesting details, anecdotes, and analyses for both admirers and critics of Stephen Harper. On balance, however, there is certainly more for those who favour him.

Harper and I first crossed paths in a sense in the 1979 general election when he lived in the riding of Edmonton-Strathcona. It was my first election campaign as a Conservative in Alberta; recently, I learned that he had not voted for me. Clearly, he was then no Tory partisan, or perhaps he simply disliked his local candidate.

Ten years later, in 1989, after having been an assistant to a Calgary Conservative member, Harper became one to Deborah Grey, who had just been elected in a by-election in northeastern Alberta as the first Reform MP. He and I chatted warmly, and it was clear that we both respected and liked one another, something possibly aided by the fact that my wife, Laura, and I attempted to welcome Grey to Ottawa in various ways.

Our paths have crossed numerous times since then as we have each approached our political lives in new roles, Harper as a Reform and then Conservative MP, and I as both a Liberal and an independent MP. While our policy views have been both divergent and similar over the years, I am pleased to note that we have maintained a relationship of personal respect.

Laureen Teskey, Harper's wife and no doubt his closest advisor, emerges favourably in the book as well. On meeting her for the first time, I was delighted to learn that she had visited about twenty African countries during an extended bus trip from Johannesburg to Cairo. Her genuine concern for the myriad victims in the ongoing crisis in Darfur quickly made an admirer out of me.

The publication of this book comes at a time when Canada's political parties are focusing their energies on election strategies and readiness. With a minority government, the historic vote of confidence in the government this spring was so close that the tie was broken by the speaker. Since the cult of personality is so prevalent in our present political environment, this biography comes at an important intersection in our national political dialogue.

At forty-five, Harper is the first leader of the opposition born in the latter half of the twentieth century and is only four years older than John F. Kennedy was when he became president of the United States in 1960. If Harper handles himself and his party well during the upcoming election campaign, it could become something of a rematch of the John Diefenbaker versus Louis St. Laurent campaign of 1957, when the younger leader from the west dislodged the other, albeit narrowly.

Harper has a master's degree in economics, and his thesis focused on the timely topic of how greatly increased government spending in the run-ups to general elections skews the business cycle. As an Albertan, his orientation has leaned toward the need for strengthening the regional contribution to a strong Canada. As leader, he has correctly focused attention on Quebec and might be able to negotiate a sustainable new accommodation between Quebec and the rest of Canada.

Contrary to partisan myth, Harper seems to have been able to maintain genuine diversity in a "big tent" party — from Peter MacKay to Bev Oda to Jim Prentice. Belinda Stronach's recent departure to the Liberal side possibly did

Harper an unintended favour by allowing him, the party, and candidates more time to prepare for the general election.

To succeed, however, Harper and his supporters must above all convince Canadians that he represents their diverse hopes, dreams, and opinions. He must force himself to keep to the high ground at all times. He must position himself and his party as close to the political centre as possible, leaving his main adversary to continue a leftward thrust. He must make it clear that Canadians can trust him to strengthen social programs as the economy grows.

Political opponents will immerse themselves in other sections of the book. Does Harper have a "secret agenda" on health care, as the Liberals and NDP claim? Why was he willing to see "Red Tories" such as Joe Clark and David Orchard leave? Why did he propose a "firewall" in 2001 by which the Alberta government could prevent federal incursions into matters falling within primarily provincial jurisdiction?

Lloyd Mackey is a knowledgeable and skilled observer of our national scene. His research is sound, and his judgments are responsible. He has done Canadians a service by writing this book.

Honourable David Kilgour, MP
June 2005

Acknowledgements

Many individuals and more than a few groups have helped to make this book a reality. I hope I can do all of them justice.

The Canadian Parliamentary Press Gallery, of which I am a member, and the Parliamentary Library provided helpful access to both Stephen Harper, the political person, and virtually everything that has been written about him in Canadian media since he first became a Member of Parliament twelve years ago.

I was able to talk to many of the people who have been close to Harper. They have shared facts, figures, and information that helped to anchor much of the book's analysis. And the fact that they also talked to William Johnson, author of *Stephen Harper and the Future of Canada*, telling him the same things that they told me, has been a source of some comfort. I trust that, seen in context, they will be able to appreciate how their particular part of the biographical tapestry contributed to the whole.

I have greatly enjoyed working with Dallas Harrison, my editor, who has a way of ensuring that my sometimes convoluted style of writing becomes miraculously clear. Additionally, he has an excellent grounding in the issues that help to shape the west and its populism.

Edna, my wife, has been a fine sounding board, a constant support, and a strong partner, both personally and in helping me to think through the things about which I write, about both politics and faith.

Introduction

Shortly after the June 28, 2004, federal election, I began exploring, with my publisher, Jack David of ECW Press, the idea of writing a book about Stephen Harper. I'd had a good experience working with Jack on *Like Father, Like Son: Ernest Manning and Preston Manning* in 1997. In a sense, I saw this book as a sequel. Manning had taken the new, western-based Reform Party from scratch to official opposition status in Ottawa in one decade. In the process, he had "discovered" Harper, mentored him in a new way of doing politics, and perhaps unwittingly prepared the way for him to emerge into the leadership role he occupies today.

Like Father, Like Son had an important faith-based element. After all, Ernest Manning, Preston's late father and Alberta premier from the mid-1940s to the late 1960s, was also an evangelical radio preacher of note and a friend of Billy Graham. Preston inherited his parents' faith, made it his own, and practised it thoughtfully, devoutly, and openly.

Manning clearly understood the concept of the separation of church and state rooted in the two-edged belief that a nation-state is not a theocracy run by the clergy and, in turn, that its religious communities should not have their beliefs and practices infringed upon. He also knew, however, that the separation of church and state did not mean the building of an impenetrable wall between people of faith and the body politic.

In fact, many of the people whom Manning mentored politically listened carefully when he talked about the potential for a healthy relationship between faith and politics. They were helped by his belief that politics, in its finest form, is the reconciliation of conflicting interests. It did not take them long to learn that Manning rested this concept on an understanding of the Christian gospel as an agency of reconciliation.

It was, in a sense, a quaint and otherworldly idea, seemingly ill suited to the parry and thrust of the adversarial system that was very much a part of parliamentary democracy. Nevertheless, Manning helped a number of the people whom he brought into the political sphere to come to faith and to bring that faith to bear on public policy issues.

When I embarked on writing this book on Harper, Jack and I discussed whether it, like *Like Father, Like Son*, might turn out to be a story of the interface of faith and politics. I was inclined to agree that such an interface existed, to a limited extent, in Harper's life and political practice. I also believed, though, that Stephen and Laureen Teskey Harper would be embarrassed if I made too much of this. After all, Preston Manning, despite his care in being more cerebral than emotive about his faith, had been ridiculed by various Liberal political competitors. And for Stockwell Day, that ridicule became both raw and explosive at times.

In the run-up to the 2004 election, Harper was quoted in *Maclean's* magazine as predicting that the Liberals would attack "my faith, my family and my party." He even became reluctant to close his speeches during that campaign with his customary request that "God bless Canada" lest he be accused of trying to make the nation into a theocracy.

After the 2004 election, I saw increasing evidence of the faith-politics interface in the larger Harper story. I saw things this way partly because of my observations of some of the polling conducted in Canada in the past ten years about the significance of faith in the lives of Canadians. In short, many of these polls indicated an interesting conundrum: while seventy percent of the population affirm a statement that strongly links their relationship with God and their personal conduct with their belief in "Christ, who lived and died and rose again," only about one quarter of that seventy percent regularly attend church. Similar statistics prevail, upon closer reflection, for people of other faiths as well.

All of the above coincided with the fact that, for thirty-seven years, my journalism has reflected a heavy emphasis on reportage and analysis of the interfaces between faith and politics and, to some extent, between faith and business. So it was natural that the same analytical processes that I applied in telling Manning's story would be useful in tracing Harper's pilgrimage. And, while I recognized that similar faith stories could be told about leaders in other parties, I realized that my own pilgrimage had well equipped me to look at contemporary conservatism in Canada through a faith-based lens.

Jack and I were aware that veteran Quebec journalist William Johnson was writing a comprehensive Harper biography particularly focusing on the Conservative leader's views on Quebec. That book, *Stephen Harper and the Future of Canada*, published by McClelland and Stewart, was released in late June 2005. Its release left me free to pursue the objective of focusing more sharply on Harper's political and spiritual pilgrimage. Furthermore, I felt free to put that pilgrimage into historical, sociological, and philosophical contexts.

Johnson compellingly tells the stories of Harper's relationship with Quebec, Brian Mulroney, Atlantic Canada, and two of the people who helped to shape his journey: Tom Flanagan and John Weissenberger. But there was an obvious need for a book that would serve a certain segment of the population. That sector includes those who see faith as relevant to politics and everyday life without the domineering or repressive downsides often seemingly related to religious activity — and who believe that conservative parties are open to such people.

I grew up in a Plymouth Brethren home in Victoria. As a young teen, I was given a little mantel radio by my parents along with some instructions that, if I was going to listen to such worldly radio programs as *The Shadow* and *Jack Benny* on a Sunday afternoon, I should also tune in to Christian programs. My three favourites were Billy Graham, Charles E. Fuller (the preacher through whom Jerry Falwell came to faith), and the premier of Alberta, Ernest Manning.

In 1979, Manning, by that time a senator, accepted an appointment as honourary chair of a Billy Graham mission to be held in Edmonton that year. I was asked by Roger Palms, then editor of Graham's *Decision* magazine, to help the former premier tell his story. At that time, Mr. Manning (only those closest to him called him Ernest) introduced me to Preston. Almost ten years later Preston asked me to edit the *Reformer*, which served as a newspaper to the new and then rapidly growing Reform Party community.

So it is that, seventeen years after the founding of the Reform Party, we can trace the political pilgrimage of Stephen Harper, weaving into the tapestry of his story both his faith and that of many of the people who trek together with him in Canada's political conservatism.

I should note that the time frame in which I conducted many of the interviews for this book was following the 2004 federal election. Hence, many of the people interviewed, even if they had been adversaries of or at odds with Harper at other times, were now pulling for him.

I interviewed Preston Manning in April 2005 and Rick Anderson, his former policy advisor, in late 2004. With both of them, I carefully approached the question of conflict between them and Harper in earlier years. For Manning, the question surrounded Harper's early return to Calgary, in 1996, to head up the National Citizens Coalition, after having been elected in 1993 as MP for Calgary West. The media reports about his departure cited tensions between Harper and Manning over Harper's belief that Manning was too populist and not conservative enough. With Anderson, the issue was that his previous Liberal background clashed too sharply with Harper's policy approaches — that Anderson was too liberal an influence on Manning. Anderson pointedly told me that the relationship between Manning and Harper was good and had been for a number of years. Indeed, he noted, Manning remains one of Harper's spiritual mentors — and, incidentally, one of Anderson's. And Manning, sensing that I was trying to probe the purported tensions, quietly diverted my thinking: "Lloyd, make this a constructive, affirming kind of book," he said. "Stephen will be a good prime minister, and I, for one, want to contribute to that affirmation."

When I wrote *Like Father, Like Son*, there were other books written at the same time about Preston. One was warmer and fuzzier than mine; another was written by a friendly critic. Still another was written by a radically left author who was quite hostile. Ironically, he even managed to write an unfriendly book about Paul Martin.

My Manning book was awarded first place in 1998 in the historical/political category in the Canadian Christian Writers' Award competition sponsored, at the time, by *Faith Today* magazine — even though the book was not "religious" per se and was not published by a religious publishing house. The judges' key comment was that I told the Manning story, neither apologizing for nor attacking the two men. And Peter C. Newman, the fearsome and famous former editor of *Maclean's*, apologized in a review run on August 11, 1997 (I can still remember the date), for having knocked Preston's faith. And the reason for the apology? Newman had read *Like Father, Like Son*.

I had no way of knowing for sure, in the spring of 2005, whether the subject of this book would soon become the next prime minister of Canada. In fact, I had some discussion with the publisher, when the book was mostly written, whether I should hurry up and finish it so that it would be available before a late-spring election, should one be called. We decided to stay with the initial game plan, to release it in October 2005, because then it would be a story about Stephen Harper that would help people to understand the man as well as provide some insight into the future of his political and faith pilgrimage.

Each chapter deals with one phase of Harper's pilgrimage, starting with his high school years and the decision, in his late teens, to move from Toronto to Calgary to work. Harper lived in a home in Toronto where his parents voted Liberal. His summers were often spent in New Brunswick with his paternal grandparents. But when he was old enough to make his own choices, he headed west to Alberta, first to work in the oil patch and then to study economics.

From Calgary, Harper made three forays east to Ottawa to toil in the political vineyard. And three times he retreated to Calgary, disillusioned by what he saw to be the mixture of turmoil, rigidity, and lethargy in that vineyard. It was not really until he worked his way through the disappointment of the 2004 election results that either he or the people working with him sensed that he was into nation-building for the long run.

CHAPTER ONE

A Leader
in the Making

While Stephen Joseph Harper himself has never exhibited particularly strong prime ministerial ambitions, a substantial number of conservative thinkers and operatives, mostly from western Canada, have been gently nudging him forward from the time he was in his mid-twenties. There were certain critical moments in that process when the leadership theme grew.

It found its inception in Harper's involvement in Progressive Conservative MP Jim Hawkes's office and riding organization in the 1980s. Harper and Cynthia Williams, his girlfriend at the time, worked as volunteers in Hawkes's riding association in Calgary West, where Hawkes was first

elected in 1979. Following his re-election in 1984, Harper
went to Ottawa to be his legislative assistant.

Harper returned to Calgary after a couple of years, frustrated with the political process. It was the first time but not,
by any means, the last that he exhibited some reluctance to
admit that he had political leadership potential. Some of his
friends wondered if he would end up permanently in the
halls of academe, preaching rather than practising the intricacies of public policy.

After returning west, Harper enrolled in the University
of Calgary, working on his M.A. in economics. (He had
completed his B.A. at the same school during his first Alberta
stint.) That was when Robert Mansell, later the head of the
university's economics department, acquiesced to Preston
Manning's request for his "brightest, young graduate student" who could assist Manning in policy formulation for
the new Reform Party, then in its founding stages. As legend
has it, Mansell walked Manning across the hall from his own
office and introduced him to Harper.

After Manning brought him onto the Reform team,
Harper ran against Hawkes in 1988, the first year the new
party fielded candidates in a federal election. Hawkes recalls
that Harper thought his political mentor would handily
defeat him — which he did.

But Harper headed back to Ottawa, working as legislative assistant for the lone Reform MP at the time, Deborah
Grey. Grey recalls him as bright, hardworking, policy oriented — and conflicted. Harper found difficult the tensions
of an MP's office, pulled as it was between listening to all
kinds of constituent concerns while trying to give leadership
on public policy issues. And he wanted to complete his

M.A., whose thesis was a sharp analysis of the tendency of governments — particularly those of interventionist bent — to spend heavily at election time, thus blunting the effectiveness of a market economy.

It was at that time that Harper found his life's partner, Laureen Teskey. She helped him to complete his thesis. But more than that, she showed a confidence in him that helped him to deal with those things that periodically conflicted him. She and their ensuing children also, according to Grey, helped him to transform from someone who appeared on the surface to be pretty much a policy wonk into a warm and compassionate, if still somewhat shy, human being. No one has ever accused Harper of being a party animal; in fact, he uses his "cool" image to some advantage when necessary.

"I don't run around on my wife," he told reporters during his bid for the Conservative leadership in 2004. The statement, in context, was meant as a tongue-in-cheek apology for not surrounding himself with enough drama to make for sensational news copy. He was not really trying to draw a moral line between himself and other politicians who might sleep around from time to time.

In 1993, Harper ran against Hawkes, winning this time and becoming part of the western sweep for Reform that played a role in wiping out Brian Mulroney's Conservatives. In effect, Harper had crossed his Rubicon. The Conservatives saw Reform as the enemy that had destroyed their party. The bitterness was deep, directed mostly at Preston Manning and, to a lesser extent, at Harper. Few except the most far-sighted would have dared to predict that the Conservative family would be back together in not much more than a decade. Even the most optimistic would not have thought that Harper would be pivotal in the process and that Mulroney and Manning, in their separate ways, would contribute to the coming together.

But there were still some hills to climb and valleys to cross for Harper. He left Parliament before the end of his first term to return to Calgary. Tension between Harper and Manning has been popularly cited as the reason. That assumption is not totally without foundation. One of the attributes that seems to make Harper a leader is that he finds it difficult to be led, though maturity and Laureen have helped him to minimize that difficulty.

This time his Calgary "parking space" was the presidency of the National Citizens Coalition, a fiscally conservative lobby group. And there in that space he remained, until the Canadian Alliance imploded under Stockwell Day's leadership.

The Day story will bear retelling some other day (pun intended). There are several conspiracy theories with respect to his rise and fall as the first Canadian Alliance leader. Each theory has some assumed credence but also includes potential for demagoguery, paranoia, and rational explanation. I will briefly state each theory.

> • The Conservatives, while willing to reunite, believed that it would be helpful to devalue Manning's creation to make the reunion more equitable. Day was seen as someone who, despite his quick study abilities and generally congenial personality, and because of his limited leadership skill sets and lack of federal experience, could accomplish that devaluation.
> • Many of Day's supporters were religious leaders

attuned to an intriguing spinoff within evangelical Christianity, which was both charismatic and theocratic in conviction. They believed that Manning's theories on the interface of faith and politics were too limited and cerebral. They hoped that the ascension of Day would mark a new sweep of God's power in the "dominion" of Canada.

• Both groups had the common belief — but for different reasons — that Manning needed to be on the sidelines before true unification could take place. Day could accomplish the removal and then pave the way for someone who could accomplish the reunification. (Ironically, Manning had sometimes articulated similar sentiments in talking about reconciliation theory. He would suggest that, when the intended reconciler finds that he or she is an obstacle to that intention, then it is time to step aside.)

There are gaps in the above theories and their various spinoffs. But they are like many urban myths: there is just enough reality to make them useful analytical tools for understanding what really happened in the years that brought a reluctant Harper back into the fray. And they provide some explanations for the ongoing potential for tension within the party that Harper stands a fair chance of leading into government.

So reluctance turned into strong interest, and Harper decided to run for the Canadian Alliance leadership against Day and "unity" candidates Diane Ablonczy and Grant Hill. He maintained that his task was to rebuild the Alliance and that there was no point in talking unity with Joe Clark's Conservatives. Once in the leader's chair, Harper lost no time in proving that point. He and Clark did have one well-publicized conversation, and it went nowhere. Harper cooled his heels on the unity front, determining to concentrate on the rebuilding task. Clark quit the Conservative leadership following the 2000 election, resigned to the fact that he would never return to the prime minister's office, which he had held briefly twenty years earlier.

Then came Peter MacKay. He took over as Conservative leader with the help of David Orchard, who wrung from him a loosely worded agreement not to have truck or trade with the Canadian Alliance. But Harper concluded, correctly, that MacKay, unlike Clark, was someone with whom he could do business. In fact, he had a few "spies" in the personhood of the several dissidents to Day's leadership who had formed a parliamentary group called the Democratic Reform, which established a coalition with Clark's Conservatives.

Once Harper was in the chair, he invited the DRs back into the Alliance caucus. They did not have to repent of their dissidence but were expected to work in common cause in healing the Alliance.

And the former DRs provided some of the espionage that Harper needed — that, indeed, the Conservatives under MacKay were amenable to unity.

Once the process of unification was under way, Harper lost his reluctance completely, replacing it with a gritty determination to pursue MacKay. His political ardour showed itself once in his hopping onto a plane, flying halfway across the country, and pinning down a face-to-face meeting with MacKay. They joked, once the merger was consummated, that it was a same-sex union of sorts.

Only once more did Harper give pause to the belief that

he was in this for the long run and was ready to replace Paul Martin as prime minister. That was right after the 2004 election. Every indication was that Harper was deeply disappointed — and once again conflicted — over losing the election. He went on a vacation with Laureen and the children and otherwise lay low for several weeks until he returned to Ottawa to name his shadow cabinet.

The common question was "Will he quit?" Underlying that query were the periodic reports that Harper was deeply depressed. His supporters say that he was not depressed, just devastated. Jay Hill, Conservative House leader, confirmed what many others had told me but not for attribution: as a person with high-achiever objectives, Harper finds it difficult to fail. "Stephen was blaming himself," Hill said. It took a while, and many people, to lift that burden of blame from him.

John Reynolds, Hill's predecessor as House leader and his campaign co-chair for the next election, put it this way: "We let him down." He did not get much more specific than that. But, as one of Harper's acknowledged sounding boards, he believed that the broad range of people who encouraged Harper soon helped him to know that he had a lot of friends.

Also implicit to Harper's recovery was the reality, after the 2004 election, that Harper at least had the second best of all worlds.

The general wisdom is that Harper would not have survived the election of a minority Conservative government because the entrenched bureaucracy, the Liberals, the NDP, and to a lesser extent the Bloc would have made his life a living hell. A majority government would have been the best option because it would have prevailed as long as he wanted it to. But opposition in a minority setting had the downside as well of disappointing some of the party's supporting fringes, because it could not accomplish everything promised or implied.

As it was, the minority was there, together with the promise of a policy convention in March 2005. Meanwhile, in setting up the shadow cabinet, Harper gave it the appearance of a real cabinet swearing-in. It was not long before the public perception was that this was a very strong front bench.

Harper did one other thing. He moved his communication director, Jim Armour, into a new post with the title of public affairs director. And he brought in the urbane and articulate Geoff Norquay to replace Armour. In his new spot, Armour has handled the longer-term task of projecting a "government-in-waiting." And part of the "waiting" process was preparing for the policy convention. (In the late spring of 2005, believing he had done what he could for the cause, Armour became communications director for the Canadian Medical Association.)

So all along the way, bits and pieces of leadership have emerged, just as a number of people had suggested, for almost two decades, they would. I will briefly mention those who take some credit for identifying Harper's political leadership potential.

• An early observer was Frank Atkins, the University of Calgary economist who supervised Harper's 1991 master's thesis, entitled "The Political Business Cycle and Fiscal Policy in Canada."
• John Reynolds watched Harper from afar for many years but became a sounding board for him when the

Conservative leader's father died in 2003. Reynolds holds the distinction of having been an MP in both the new Conservative party and the Progressive Conservative '70s caucuses of Robert Stanfield and Joe Clark. He predicts that Harper will be a prime minister in the vein of Pierre Elliott Trudeau. The obvious question to Reynolds, of course, is how Harper, a classic conservative, can be compared with that man who, whatever his strengths, had a definite leftist tilt and wielded his influence with flamboyant arrogance rather than quiet determination. Reynolds' reply is that Harper has a mind every bit as analytical as Trudeau's, he knows what he wants, and he works at maintaining his integrity.

• Deborah Grey sat alone as a Reform MP before the "Class of '93" was elected, and Harper was her legislative assistant.

• Edmonton independent MP and former Liberal cabinet minister David Kilgour says that Harper's "prudent use of words" is one of his strengths. Kilgour is obviously one of Harper's fans, perhaps partly because Kilgour himself was a Conservative before turning Liberal in the early 1990s. He admits that Harper's clear, cool way of thinking and speaking will stand him in good stead should he become prime minister.

• Gordon Shaw, the first executive director of the Reform Party, back in the early 1990s, first saw Harper's leadership potential when Harper made the closing speech at Reform's benchmark Winnipeg Assembly in 1987.

• Robert Harper, one of his accountant brothers, followed Stephen as legislative assistant in Grey's office and is now a Calgary-based financial executive for a major food chain. He says his brother has been reluctant to aspire to leadership despite his self-assurance and natural bent for organizing people and projects.

• Robert Mansell, as head of the University of Calgary economics department, introduced Harper to Preston Manning.

As we progress through the chapters, we will trace the ebb and flow of Harper's public life to date. Out of those meanderings, we will try to figure out the occasional conundrums that his particular style and substance could bring to the prime minister's mantle, should it fall upon him.

CHAPTER TWO

The Apprenticeship

If Stephen Harper becomes prime minister, he will be the first to be born in the second half of the twentieth century. Thus, he will be well removed from the direct influences of World War II and the Great Depression. In fact, he was only a few months old when the 1960s were thrust upon us. April 20, 1959, is the exact date that Margaret Harper gave birth to little Stephen Joseph in Toronto.

Four years later Jean Chrétien was elected for the first time to the House of Commons. And, in the spring of 2002, Harper faced him for the first time as opposition leader. In welcoming him to the House, Chrétien congratulated him, wished him a long career in opposition, and noted that he was the eighth leader to face him in that spot. Harper had a

11

pretty good rejoinder. He spoke of having watched Chrétien on television when the prime minister had first entered the House, forty years before when Harper himself was just four. He suggested that he had looked up from the screen that long-ago day and declared, "Mom, someone has to do something to stop that guy!"

Harper has roots in Atlantic, central, and western Canada. His grandparents came from New Brunswick, and he sometimes spent part of his summers there as a boy. He grew up in Leaside, a Toronto suburb, and later in Etobicoke. His parents, Joseph (Joe) and Margaret Harper, provided a stable home for him and his brothers, Robert and Grant. They attended church at Leaside United, an influence that augmented the middle-of-the-road attitude at home. (The senior Harpers voted Liberal when they lived in Ontario.) Joseph, an accountant in private practice (later he held a senior accounting position at Imperial Oil), was a sounding board for Stephen right up to his death in 2003. Harper doesn't talk about his father much, but he does note occasionally, with a touch of sadness, that he misses him.

Gordon Shaw, an executive colleague at Imperial Oil, recalls Joseph's references to his "headstrong" son. Shaw maintains that the epithet was uttered as much in admiration as in frustration. Indeed, there are various reports about Harper's natural inclination to lead and equally natural disinclination to be led for more than relatively short periods.

Robert Harper says that, during his high school years, Stephen gravitated toward leadership in the organizing of his peers in the neighbourhood. He invariably took the initiative, Robert recalls.

Shaw says that, when he himself was executive director of

the Reform Party and Harper was formulating policy for Preston Manning, a frustrated Harper one day came into his office and stated that he did not like "being told what to do." Harper himself admits to that trait in his acknowledgements at the beginning of his master's thesis. He says there that his supervisor, Frank Atkins, "demonstrated both consistent interest and flexible accommodation while overseeing this work. He went to considerable pains to keep on track *a difficult student* who frequently had other pressing priorities" (emphasis added).

Much has been made of the apparent tensions between Manning and Harper during Reform's first term in the House of Commons beginning in 1993. Rick Anderson, a longtime campaign advisor to Manning, examines the tension in a relatively positive light. When Harper was a freshman MP, he worked long hours in his Ottawa office, Anderson says. During that time, he would have late-evening conversations with some of his Reform colleagues. "He was a good listener," Anderson says, adding that he listened to the complaints of other MPs who believed they were not getting fair access to the leader or the "insiders" in the caucus. One needed to keep in mind, Anderson suggests, that it was a new caucus with a fair number of independent thinkers who had not quite figured out the need for party discipline. Manning had to grapple with that problem, and there was some sense in the leader's office and among the caucus officers that maintaining that discipline was a bit like herding cats.

So for Harper an informal leadership role was emerging as the new party was finding its feet. He was in the right place, in an office just around the corner from that of the leader, accessible to many of his fellow MPs. Even though newly married, Harper kept long hours on the Hill. Not being a party type, he had a door open during those evenings to anyone who wanted to drop by to talk policy or politics or simply to complain or commiserate.

Jay Hill, MP from Prince George–Peace River in central British Columbia, was one of those colleagues. His late-night conversations with Harper can be seen in the context of his own ability to work with the various party strands with a fair level of integrity.

Later Hill kept himself available to Manning during the Day reign. He became a dissident and went through the PC-DR parliamentary coalition experience. During his exile from the Canadian Alliance, he turned up to give moral support to Diane Ablonczy when she declared her "unity" candidacy for the CA leadership. Ablonczy herself came just centimetres from joining the dissidents but decided to remain on board the Alliance ship.

Once Harper became leader and invited the dissidents back, with only a tight timeline as a condition, Hill was there. In due course, after the CA-PC merger, he became party whip. And when John Reynolds retired as House leader, so that he could co-chair the next election campaign, Hill succeeded him. He likes to think, and is probably justified in doing so, that his time in exile, working alongside the PCs, prepared him for the House leader's role, because he had taken the risks necessary to understand the cultures of both parties.

Harper's 1993–97 stint as MP was the penultimate leg of his leadership apprenticeship, which began when Harper was a high school student in Etobicoke and, according to his brother Robert, the organizer of many neighbourhood projects and activities. Not that he found this apprenticeship easy. His headstrong attitude, the impatience that kept him bouncing between Calgary and Ottawa every few years, his self-admitted "difficult student" status that plagued him as he tried to complete his master's thesis — these were the characteristics that needed honing if Harper was to become the leader that others were expecting him to be.

* * *

Even the struggle that moved Harper from religious scepticism to a strong, cerebral Christian faith represents a chapter in his leadership development. A significant aspect of biblically based leadership development is the concept that a good leader must first be a good servant. (Jesus talked about this idea in a leadership development session with his twelve disciples. Mark 9:35 notes that, sitting down with them, he said, "If anyone wants to be first, he must be the very last, and the servant of all.")

In contemporary Christian leadership development theory, the servant leadership concept — that one earns the right to lead through good servanthood — is, in a sense, a paradox. A servant leader does not force his or her values on society but finds ways to serve society so as to win legitimate acceptance of those values. Christian thought is not, of course, the sole repository of servant leadership theory. The point here is that, while Harper was honing his leadership skills, he was willing to let his faith instincts guide him.

* * *

When Harper moved from Toronto to Calgary to begin his study of economics at the University of Calgary, he had no way of knowing that the move would be significant to his assuming leadership of a party that had, along with the nation's population, moved its centre of gravity somewhat west. There was a time, well before Harper was born, that Montreal was Canada's largest city and home to many corporate headquarters. Toronto, six hours' drive to the west, was second by population and corporate office count. By the time Harper was growing up in Leaside and Etobicoke, Toronto had overtaken its francophone counterpart.

One significant reason for this shift was Quebec's "Quiet Revolution," which made life uncomfortable for the anglophone elites in Montreal as the francophone majority struggled for ascendancy in "their own land." But something else was happening as well. The west was emerging from the dual impacts of the drought of the 1930s and the Great Depression.

The economic injection brought on by World War II helped to overcome the basic economic problems, but in a disruptive and painful way, and the political antidotes to those impacts were the populist parties. There were the left-leaning Liberals-Progressives and Cooperative Commonwealth Federation in Manitoba and Saskatchewan respectively. In Alberta and later in British Columbia, the more conservative Social Credit emerged.

These regional parties would never become national entities of any significance unless they threw in with their national counterparts. The CCF morphed into the New Democratic Party by broadening its agrarian base to include the eastern labour unions. The national wing of the Progressives went in with the Conservatives when former Manitoba premier John Bracken became the Conservative leader in 1942. The Liberals-Progressives governed in

Manitoba for another two decades. They were informally known as Liberals, but the Progressive element dominated the party.

Ironically, but not undeservedly, their premier from 1948 to 1958, Douglas Campbell, was honoured with the first-ever Bridge-Builders Award at the 1991 Reform Assembly in Saskatoon, at age ninety-five. The citation was for his long-term commitment to building "bridges" in previously uncharted political territories so that younger successors would not have to span the chasms unaided.

The Saskatoon Assembly was where, at thirty-two, Stephen Harper's speech captured the attention of Laureen Teskey. Her heart was soon to follow. She took some initiatives to get to know him better. He responded in kind. Maybe Campbell's bridge was meant for them.

All of which returns us to Harper's apprenticeship. During his teen years, Harper admired Trudeau. It was a natural thing to do. His parents, like many longtime central and eastern Canadian residents, leaned Liberal. Any sense of western alienation and the kind of conservatism that it could spawn was vague.

In 1979, having graduated from Etobicoke's Richview Collegiate with a gold medal for highest marks, Harper responded to the "Go west, young man!" call that continuously lured easterners to the Alberta oil patch. He might have been acting from an inside tip of sorts. By that time, his father was a senior accountant at Imperial Oil's headquarters in Toronto and himself in line for a possible move west. Stephen worked at various jobs in Alberta, mostly in the computer programming field, for Imperial Oil and other companies.

That was when the Harper family's Toronto-based Liberal bent began to morph, for Stephen, into a more conservative understanding of economics. He was working in Alberta when Pierre Trudeau, having just defeated the short-lived Joe Clark Conservative government, introduced the National Energy Program. While it was ostensibly meant to stabilize domestic oil supplies and prices, the NEP was enormously devastating both to the Alberta economy and to the Canadian oil industry. Westerners saw it as a $60 billion cash grab, which only reinforced the already prevailing view that the west was a goblet intended to be drained by eastern corporate interests.

His work helped to steer Harper to the University of Calgary, where he earned his bachelor's degree in economics in 1985. And it got him involved in political activity. He became youth campaign chair for the Calgary West Progressive Conservative Association. In that spot, he was witness to the Brian Mulroney Tory sweep of 1984. And once his degree was behind him, he accepted an offer from Jim Hawkes, who had won the Calgary West seat, to be his legislative assistant in Ottawa. A year later, though, Harper was back in Calgary, apparently disillusioned since Mulroney appeared to be helpless to rein in the ballooning deficit created by Trudeau.

In talking about the master's degree studies that gave Harper the grounding to move forward, University of Calgary economist Frank Atkins, who supervised Harper's thesis, noted that the 2004 election gave Canadians a chance to see the difference between Paul Martin, committed to a command economy approach, and Harper, who, in his view, grasped how various market and government forces work to grow an economy.

Harper produced an economic statement for campaign purposes that proposed certain decreases in tax rates and increases in social spending. Both Paul Martin and Minister of Finance Ralph Goodale immediately attacked the statement, thundering that it contained a "$50 billion hole." Atkins suggested that Martin won that little skirmish by "blustering." Atkins admitted the difficulty of getting people to understand that a reduction in tax *rates*, under the right circumstances, increases tax *revenues* because the stimulus to the economy from the rate cut will result in more revenue. That is why social spending, under such circumstances, can be increased. The Martin-Goodale bluster contributed considerably to the collapse of the Conservative campaign in 2004, Atkins suggested. Yes, the socons and their off-message statements about abortion and gay rights amplified almost daily by a "Liberal hegemony" were of no help to the Conservatives. But Atkins predicted that Harper's staying the course on economic and tax issues, while remaining realistic on social spending, would serve him well in the quest for a Conservative government.

Robert Mansell, the University of Calgary professor (head of the economics department at the time) who introduced Harper to Preston Manning, tells of getting to know the young graduate student after he returned in frustration from his Ottawa stint with Hawkes. Ottawa was, for Harper, "too random and politically expedient." Mansell suggests, with some satisfaction, that he helped to "discover" that Harper has a unique grasp of Canada's political and economic history — including the twin issues of Quebec and western alienation.

The courses that Harper took for his master's degree provided him with an analytical approach. Mansell says that his student had a way of separating policy issues into bite-size chunks, so that, when he got into brainstorming and idea-bouncing sessions with colleagues or fellow students, the discussions were generally productive and useful.

Manning, meanwhile, was building the new Reform movement, and it was reaching a point where it needed a little more mind power. "He came to my office and said, 'We need someone who will take us to the next policy level,'" Mansell recalls, allowing that even then Harper was "a reluctant politician — an ideal politician in my sense." But reluctant or not Harper was able to work his grasp of economics into clear policy statements and questions for Manning to move forward. And, in Mansell's view, he did not make any big mistakes as he inched forward into elective politics. "He was always a very reasonable person."

But at the same time, Harper knows how to pose the right questions from a western perspective. True, Alberta, as a have province, may need to send money to Ottawa. But Harper knows how to ask tough and embarrassing questions about how it would use that money.

And Mansell puts forward the theme that timing on the health care debate is just one example of the formidable task Harper would face as prime minister. Mansell suggests, "You can't have a good debate on the subject, because it is dominated by emotional reaction," based on the common fear that economic conservatives are too "pro-American."

Part of what could happen with Harper leading the country, Mansell suggests, is a "cultural shift." A prime minister who is good at analysing past and potential policies will know what he "can and cannot do" and what the country can do "really well." And he suggests that with Harper "it is not an insurmountable challenge."

All of these "apprenticeship" issues and items need to be assessed in light of the particular way in which Harper's mind works, for beneath his dull exterior is a way of, so to speak, seeing around corners. In the next chapter, we will explore that mind a little more.

CHAPTER THREE

Beneath That
Dull Exterior

More than a few observers have said that Stephen Harper presents a dull image. But he has a warmth that many who watch carefully for it are able to glimpse fleetingly. And some — such as Diane Ablonczy and Jim Hawkes — have experienced it in fair measure, perhaps when least expected.

I should note, parenthetically, that I was bound by Harper's decision not to permit formal, one-on-one interviews with prospective biographers because he did not want to "scoop" himself should he decide to write a book of his own. I found the decision to be prudent perhaps and at the least understandable. But as a journalist working on Parliament Hill, I had relatively good access to him and fair opportunities to observe him closely, as he worked, without him being aware of my presence.

Furthermore, since my wife is an administrative assistant to a Conservative MP, I had many occasions, as a dutiful spouse, to attend Hill gatherings where Stephen and Laureen were "working the room." While he tended to hang back and let people cluster around him, Laureen plunged into the crowd and took the initiative in establishing contact and conversation. But they were both equally warm and showed aptitude for listening carefully — and later remembering those conversations and their contexts.

One event provided an excellent observation post for me as both journalist and spouse. Each year both the prime minister and the opposition leader invite members of the press gallery (there are over four hundred of us) to their respective official Ottawa residences for an informal and ostensibly off-the-record mixer.

In the early fall after the 2004 election, Stephen and Laureen hosted the gallery at Stornoway, the opposition leader's residence. Instead of inviting just the gallery, they encouraged them to bring along their spouses and children.

It proved to be a memorable evening with good vibes for the various shapes and shades of family that turned up. It helped, of course, that a big rubber bouncing castle had been set up in the Harper backyard, and Laureen enthusiastically told stories and handed out dishes of ice cream to the dozens of kids on hand. And Rachel and Benjamin Harper had no trouble making many new friends that evening.

Harper, for his part, was cool and relaxed, as if he had no worry in the world. No anger or dour countenance in evidence that evening.

In the early days of Reform, when Ablonczy was a recent young widow and the single parent of a difficult-to-handle teenage daughter, Harper spent a fair amount of time listening to her. Considerably younger though he was, he seemed to understand her situation, she recalls, perhaps because he knew that his own headstrong attitude as a teenager had given his parents a few moments of concern. Years later, now married to Ron Sauer, a Calgary agricultural implement salesman, Ablonczy recalls the attention paid by Harper in helping her through those difficult months. (Today she is on good terms with her daughter and enjoys being a grandmother.)

And his political mentor-cum-rival, Hawkes, speaks with slightly harnessed warm emotion about Harper visiting him almost every day in the hospital when he experienced a life-threatening illness during his last term as an MP, in the early 1990s. Those hospital visits cemented, for Hawkes, a respect for the younger aspiring politician that overcame, for the most part, the tensions that their political rivalry would bring. Again it was Harper's skill of listening that helped.

At that time, Hawkes and Harper had one political contest behind them. In 1988, Harper had run against the incumbent Conservative as a candidate in the embryonic Reform party. As the younger man had expected, he had lost, but he saw the experience as one in which he had tested his political and policy mettle. Harper had visited Hawkes and told him he wanted to run. Hawkes had given him his blessing, perhaps knowing even then that the mentor-to-rival transition had begun and likely would not end with that election.

And neither did it. Harper defeated Hawkes in the 1993

election that saw the Conservatives reduced to two seats. The former Hawkes aide became one of the "Class of '93" that put Reform on the federal map and gave the young economist another leg up, should he ever overcome his reluctance about leadership.

Hawkes, who holds a Ph.D. from Colorado State University in experimental psychology, worked — along with his wife, Joanne — with the Westmount YMCA in Montreal in the late 1950s, during his time as a student at Sir George Williams University. Once back in Calgary, his hometown, he held teaching, counselling, and administrative positions at Mount Royal College and later the University of Calgary.

But it was his political activity that both prepared him to be one of Harper's first political mentors and placed him in the right place at the right time to do so. Hawkes's official political initiation came when Joe Clark started calling when he was considering a run at the Progressive Conservative leadership. When Clark won the leadership — and with it the opposition leader's post — he asked Hawkes to join him in Ottawa to become his program director. In 1979, Hawkes ran for the Tories in Calgary West and held the seat until Harper defeated him in 1993.

During his Ottawa tenure, Hawkes was parliamentary secretary in 1988–89 to the deputy prime minister of the day, Don Mazankowski — one of the "emissaries" who helped to cobble together the Alliance-Tory merger for Harper and MacKay in 2003. From 1988 to 1993, Hawkes was the Conservative whip. His task, ironically, was to keep the 169-member Tory caucus in line on the government side while, across the aisle, Deborah Grey, the original Reform MP, toiled alone, with Harper working as her legislative assistant.

In the early 1980s, Harper and Cynthia Williams, a young journalism student, began dating. She recalls that he was a "great boyfriend," but their idea of fun was not noisy partying. Their preferred activities were watching movies with friends, visiting the zoo, and volunteering for political activities.

As it happened, they became involved in Hawkes's Calgary West Conservative riding association. Hawkes recalls them first turning up at coffee parties, where they spoke up and asked questions. That led to committee work, which they undertook, sometimes as a couple and sometimes separately. Harper became president, at one point, of a strong youth wing in the riding. Hawkes suggests that Harper's social skills were "not the greatest," but Harper made up for it by being bright and reliable.

This was a time of philosophical metamorphosis for Harper that had likely begun with his decision to move from Toronto to Edmonton after high school to work in the oil patch.

* * *

In his home in Toronto, the politics were Liberal in a rather gentle and sedate establishment way. Coincidentally, the church of choice in the Harper home was United. When the rest of the Harper family moved west, they shifted to the somewhat more conservative Presbyterian brand. Harper, while still sometimes identifying himself religiously as Presbyterian, has chosen to worship in churches linked with one of Presbyterianism's evangelical spinoffs, the Christian and Missionary Alliance.

Certainly, the political atmosphere in Alberta was more conservative than in the Toronto in which Harper grew up. It had been shaped by the twenty-five-year Social Credit premiership of Ernest Manning, whose government had been conservative in everything but party name. The transition of Alberta from Socred to true-blue Conservative, after the retirement of the senior Manning and the emergence of Peter Lougheed as premier, took place in 1971. It was pretty much coincidental with the rollover of the federal Socreds into the Conservatives after Robert Stanfield became Tory leader.

That rollover, in fact, stopped the Socred-Conservative vote splitting in the west, leading to a strong contingent of Alberta and B.C. Conservatives going to Ottawa in the 1972 election. Twelve years and two more leadership changes later, the massive 1984 Tory win brought Brian Mulroney to power. Jim Hawkes was part of that government, and Stephen Harper was his Ottawa parliamentary assistant.

But in the 1970s, when Trudeau was still reigning and the Tory momentum was slowly building, Harper was transitioning into high school at Richview Collegiate, in a fairly tony part of Etobicoke, a western Toronto suburb. At Richview, he was an honours student and class valedictorian. And his high school yearbook predicted that he would be taking up commerce and law studies at the University of Toronto.

A June 19, 2004, profile in the *Calgary Herald*, by Michelle Lang and Suzanne Wilton, said fellow Richview students recall Harper as a reserved, thoughtful, and strong student.

"He wasn't the coolest, wackiest kid in the class," recalls high school buddy Raymond Zenkovich, now a Toronto real estate developer. Zenkovich provides some hint of unspecified political interest. He says Harper, signing his yearbook, wrote, "Good luck. I'll see you on the election trail." That was just months before Joe Clark became prime minister in 1979.

* * *

Harper, although working on his undergrad economics degree at the University of Calgary (he had a 4.0 grade-point average), was heavily involved in Hawkes's campaign for re-election in 1984. Hawkes was impressed enough with Harper that he asked him to work with him in Ottawa.

So Harper did his first stint in the capital when Brian Mulroney led the Tories into government with a whopping 211 seats out of 282. But Harper stayed there just over a year, seemingly disillusioned. He now refers to that stint as part of his "tortured political past."

Back in Calgary by 1986, Harper concluded that the Mulroney government had failed to change the basic direction of the country or to make the west a full partner in Confederation. In effect, the Mulroney Progressive Conservatives were not as conservative as he believed they needed to be.

Within months, Preston Manning was putting together this new thing called the Reform Party of Canada. (In fact, early worksheets distributed by Manning to the curious carried the moniker Western Reform Party.)

And Harper, his relationship with Williams now ended, had begun work on his master's degree at the University of Calgary, where Manning, with the help of Robert Mansell, head of the economics department, discovered him and quickly recruited him to help write policy for the new party. How different things might now be if Harper had studied at the University of Toronto or stayed on in Ottawa with Hawkes.

Hawkes recalls Harper making it "crystal clear" during his time of working with him that he would never run for public office. But Hawkes himself was not so sure that the decision was final. He was pleased, in fact, that Harper let him know ahead of time that he was going to run against him, for Reform, in Calgary West in the 1988 federal election. Reform had certainly captured his interest, and Harper saw it as reflecting the kind of western fiscal conservatism that had become part of his core value system.

Incidentally, Conservative House leader Jay Hill (Prince George–Peace River) notes that Harper and he are two of only four MPs left who ran unsuccessfully for Reform in that 1988 election. The other two are John Cummins from Delta–Richmond East and Werner Schmidt of Kelowna–Lake Country. But Schmidt had a political life even before running in 1988 for Reform. From 1973 to 1975, he had been leader of the once-mighty Alberta Social Credit Party but had been unable to restore it to the grandeur of its Ernest Manning days. Subsequently, he had been a successful educational administrator at Lethbridge Community College, the University of Lethbridge, and, after moving to the Okanagan, Okanagan University College.

But back to Harper and the 1988 election. Hawkes's protegé wondered if he should wait and perhaps run in a riding in which he would not be competing with Hawkes. Hawkes recalls that he said, simply, "Don't wait." For him, the fact that his protegé would choose to talk with him about running against him was an indication of his good manners, sense of duty, and care for others.

Indeed, that sense of duty, especially when actions might hurt someone whom Harper cares for or respects, is an important facet of his decision-making approach. But he is also able to compartmentalize to some extent personal and political questions, and he realizes that, once a decision has been made, he needs to get on with life.

After his loss to Hawkes in the 1988 election, Harper moved back to Ottawa in 1989 to work as Grey's legislative assistant. So he was on the opposite side of the political fence from Hawkes. Relations between Conservative and Reform politicians were quite caustic during that period and for some years afterward, but Hawkes held no personal bitterness. He lay low through the years of Conservative-Reform-Alliance tension and quite happily became part of the new party.

Nor did Cynthia Williams harbour any bitterness. In fact, she takes credit for introducing Harper to Laureen Teskey. (So, as it happens, do several other people. When their stories are compared, it turns out that each of them is telling part of the truth.) Williams made it a point to take credit for her part in kick-starting the Teskey-Harper duo when talking to reporters when she showed up at the 2005 Conservative convention in Montreal as a delegate from one of the Calgary ridings.

* * *

After leaving politics, Hawkes spent a few more years in college administrative work and then learned to curl and golf. He manages a faith linkage as well, attending Grace Presbyterian Church, where his wife, Joanne, is a member. And there, on occasion, during the coffee break after Sunday morning service, he will talk politics with Jim Prentice, Conservative MP for Calgary Centre-North. In fact, just days before my interview with Hawkes (two months before the Montreal policy convention), Prentice was widely quoted as saying he believes, as does Grace Presbyterian, that marriage is between a man and a woman, but . . . And the "but" is that he was going to vote for the Liberal redefinition of marriage on human rights grounds.

Prentice's announcement triggered a pastoral statement by his — and Hawkes's — minister, Victor Kim, who noted that the Presbyterian Church in Canada is on record as maintaining a male-female definition of marriage. "But the church is not a monolith," Kim added, citing the example of his erstwhile MP-parishioner Prentice. Kim used the statement as an occasion to announce Prentice's wish to have a meeting with fellow church members who wanted to provide some input on the subject.

For his part, wrapping up the "what goes around comes around" story about his friendship with Harper, Hawkes, now seventy-one, stated his satisfaction with the balance of delegates for the Montreal convention coming from his old riding. Out of forty, he noted, three or four were social conservatives. Admitting that there had been some fear of a hostile takeover of the delegate selection process by the socons, Hawkes was now quite relieved. He believed that the new party was showing the "big tent" approach that a conservative party should. And that was good.

* * *

One of a journalist's occupational hazards is retaining the essential accuracy of his or her subject's views of issues, particularly if those views need to be reduced from, say, twenty thousand words to five thousand words. It is helpful to keep that hazard in mind when reading this section.

Harper's economics master's thesis, written in 1991, runs to about 100,000 words. It is written both clearly and tightly. Furthermore, his arguments are cogent and reasoned. He wastes few words. His thesis supervisor, Frank Atkins, suggests that Harper's work was considered by his teachers as a cut or two above average. His grasp of economics, with respect to both theory and strategy, seemed to confirm what others were saying: this fellow had something to say and a way of saying it that hinted at future leadership potential.

In reading Harper's thesis, one senses the strong grounding he had already, back in 1992, in fiscal conservatism, rooted as it is in a preference for market — not command — economics. And when the $4.6 billion Liberal-NDP C-48 amendment to the 2005 federal budget was introduced in the House of Commons, it was easy to see Harper's doctrinaire rejection in the light of that academic grounding. Less economically aware Conservative leaders may well have succumbed to attempts by Paul Martin to form a de facto NDP-Grit-Tory budget coalition in the interests of "making Parliament work." But now the more mature "difficult student" could not bring himself to cooperate with what he was truly convinced was a "deal with the devil."

* * *

My own experience with the Tom Flanagan–Stephen Harper combo, when they were writing policy for the Reform Party, was that, while what they said was often long, their writing wasted no words. As editor of the *Reformer* newspaper, I had to shrink the copy for the sake of readers who could stand a thousand words but not five thousand. So, in talking about Harper's master's thesis, I have a certain sense of déjà vu.

The thesis is worth exploring because, in short, it presents the concept that governments spend money in the run-ups to elections so as to skew the natural business cycle that is part of a healthy market economy. It is that kind of thinking that leads many fiscal conservatives to view with interest the idea that Harper could become the first prime minister who is an economist. Most prime ministers have been lawyers. Paul Martin has a legal education but has been a businessman.

People with strong backgrounds in economics, particularly if they are fiscally conservative, argue against governments skewing the business cycle, either with strong intervention in the economy or with pre-election spending. They insist that such intervention represents a mistrust of normal markets and an overreliance on what they call "command and control" economics.

Political aficionados and journalists will frequently note with interest — and occasional scepticism — that governments often step up their spending in the run-ups to elections. Generally, left-leaning governments have been open and vigorous about the practice, especially as it relates to boosting social programs that arguably might prove popular with voters. Right-leaning governments, given to the principles governing a market (as opposed to a command) economy, are more critical of the practice. That is not to say they would refrain from it if push came to shove. Certainly, in political parties composed of, among others, fiscal and progressive conservatives, there is a running discussion about how much government spending should impact an economy — or the political mood — in the run-up to an election.

In effect, Harper examined in his thesis what he called the "political business cycle." He focused on Canadian federal budgets from 1953 to 1990, using what he called a "multivariate reaction function" as a measuring tool. So what was he trying to measure? He was operating from the premise that "Keynesian fiscal policy is subject to the influence of political parameters that lessen its effectiveness as a stabilization tool." But this premise was based on an assumption. In the abstract to his thesis, Harper framed the assumption thus: "Policymakers are motivated by political goals, in particular, electoral goals, rather than the social optima assumed by traditional macroeconomic policy prescriptions."

Reporting from his observations, Harper suggested that "countercyclical and electoral elements emerge as the most important factors in explaining fiscal policy. While the electoral factor represents a major constraint upon the practice of appropriate fiscal policy, the results tend not to support the premise of deliberate electoral engineering predicted by theory."

The history of twentieth-century fiscal practices in North America, as well as his personal background, helps to shape the relevance of what Harper was writing in 1991 to what he might do if he becomes Canada's first economist–prime minister.

Harper introduced his thesis with the words "Fiscal policy since Keynes has been justified on three premises: that economic fluctuations are largely a consequence of systematic instability in market behavior; that it is desirable for governments to overcome these fluctuations; and that governments are capable of correcting such instability." He then cut to the chase by noting that

> all three of these premises have come under increasing attack from economic "conservatives." Rational expectations theorists argue that markets have an inherent tendency toward stable behavior, and that any instability must be unexpected, unsystematic and therefore no basis for economic policy. Monetarists argue that fiscal policy is subject to unavoidable lags that make it inappropriate as a stabilization tool, even under the restricted circumstance for which it is suited. Public choice scholars argue that governments by their structural nature are inherently incapable of implementing correct fiscal policy.

Harper then moved on to the target of his thesis. "The most striking challenge to the view (that inappropriate policy is the erroneous action of a neutral and exogenous governmental actor) is the theory of the 'political business cycle' (PBC). According to PBC theory, modern governments may deliberately manipulate the economy not to dampen business cycles, but to create them in line with their electoral goals."

Now, a fair amount of Harper's terminology represents unfamiliar territory for the average reader of a political biography — even one about an economist-turned-politician. But bear with me, and we will soon work our way through the paper trail.

The business cycle is a familiar term in economics. It refers, in short, to the concept that a whole lot of factors, such as supply, demand, prices, wages, competition, monopoly, and so on, work together to create a cycle in which business and the economy interact with society and its households in an efficient manner. This interaction works, hopefully, as the relationships among all these factors keep moving toward equilibrium. Conservative economists maintain that the moves toward equilibrium created in the markets lead to economic stability.

* * *

The historical part of the analysis of Harper's thesis relates to a brief summary of John Maynard Keynes and his impact on American fiscal and economic practice in the twentieth century. And we look at it as seen through the eyes of Canadian-born Harvard professor John Kenneth Galbraith, who was one of Keynes's disciples during the American presidency of Franklin D. Roosevelt. (This synopsis is based, for the most part, on a September 28, 2000, Public Broadcasting Service interview with Galbraith, then ninety-two, headlined "Commanding Heights.")

Keynes's main period of influence on American economics was in the first half of the twentieth century. His hypothesis was that governments are able and willing to correct the perceived systemic instability in market behaviour. In the mid-1930s, a number of young economists, including Galbraith, were looking for a cure to the Depression. As Galbraith notes, "We were writing a book which was faithfully orthodox. It argued that the Depression was the result of the modern corporation taking control of the prices and employment and restricting in a monopolist way and leaving people outside. . . . [Then] I read [Keynes's] *The General*

Theory and recognized that our book . . . was inconsistent at the opposite extreme from [Keynes]." So off Galbraith went, for a year, to study under — and get a "sense of hope" from — Keynes.

Although Roosevelt never outwardly became a Keynesian, Galbraith says that the president was open to borrowing money, accumulating debt, hiring people across the country, and resisting conservative economic ideas. And things gradually improved — but not to the extent that they did at the onset of World War II. Says Galbraith, "We entered the war with massive unemployment, general hardship, and a very weak, ineffective economy. . . . Then came the war, public borrowing on a vast scale, public employment stimulating private employment, a return to full employment, a return to the problem with which I was overwhelmingly concerned, that of inflation."

Galbraith says that Keynes's last two major contributions to the postwar economic influences were the International Monetary Fund and the World Bank. And Keynes, after his death, became an institution of sorts — Keynesian economics. "It collected the whole liberal left movement in the United States. That became part of the accepted policy, the accepted doctrine."

Galbraith's reference to the "liberal left" offers a small clue to what was revolving around Harper by the early 1990s. In Canada, even more so than in the United States, the influences of command economy thinking — the idea that market behaviour was unstable (read "bad") and that government corrections were stabilizing (read "good") — were pretty much entrenched. Conservative Prime Minister John Diefenbaker was a fiscal progressive. He envisioned, for example, a massive government-directed redevelopment of northern Canada.

His Liberal successor, Lester Pearson, was a classic liberal with a strong international network growing out of his pre-political diplomatic service. And his successor, Pierre Elliott Trudeau, was quite left-leaning before he entered the House of Commons — indeed, a supporter of the New Democratic Party. He began a process of deficit building in Canada that his Conservative successor, Brian Mulroney, was unable to reverse despite the best efforts of his several finance ministers.

It was left to Paul Martin, as finance minister under Jean Chrétien, to turn an annual deficit of over $40 billion, within seven years, into a surplus that last year amounted to $9 billion. But it was on a regimen mostly of increased taxation that the reversal took place rather than on policies that would have reduced state spending and nudged more economic activity into the nongovernment sector.

* * *

That, then, sets the pace for a return to what Stephen Harper was writing in 1991. Bear in mind that his parents had grown up in an era of Depression and war — the same one in which Galbraith was influential as a young Keynesian economist — and, like many Torontonians, voted Liberal as long as they lived there.

Harper had little reason to question the economic status quo until he moved to Alberta, worked in the oil patch, became interested in politics, studied economics, and had his first frustrating experience as a transplanted westerner working in Ottawa.

Alberta and, to a lesser extent, British Columbia operated

in a much more fiscally conservative, private sector–invigorated economy than their more eastern counterparts. Conservative-type governments tended to operate in a relatively low-tax regime. State spending was inclined to follow revenue, rather than outpace it, so debt accumulation was considerably less a proportion of gross provincial product than in more eastern — and more liberal — provinces.

True, Alberta had oil, and British Columbia periodically succumbed to the electoral lures of the NDP. But the default position was a more fiscally conservative approach that often lined up with economic sentiments that prevailed south of the border as Keynesian influence gradually took a back seat to Reaganomics and an invigorated private sector.

In the process, the University of Calgary was developing economics and political science faculties, some of whose teachers, at least, were reflective of the local culture. And think-tanks such as the Fraser Institute and the Canada West Foundation were providing a useful research and communications backdrop to the political scene.

Furthermore, the federal Conservatives were benefiting from the success of friendly governments of long standing in both the far western provinces.

All of this gave Harper a chance to grow in his adopted but natural habitat and, as opportunities presented themselves, to take his emerging ideas east from time to time to see how they flew. Each excursion east brought him a little further into the leadership structure of Canada. And each time he ventured to Ottawa, he stayed a little longer and moved another step or two up the ladder.

Even before Harper had finished his master's studies, he was showing signs of a deep grasp of the issues that could either reinforce or undermine the sense among many of those close to him that he had a significant leadership role to play in Canada.

It was four years earlier, in fact, at Reform's October 30–November 1, 1987, founding assembly in Winnipeg, that Harper's potential leadership started to show. The Winnipeg Assembly, at which the Reform Party moved from dream to reality, took place six months after the Vancouver Assembly, which launched the movement toward party status.

Gordon Shaw, a former accountant colleague of Harper's father at Imperial Oil, was one of Preston Manning's early co-labourers in Reform. He was the party's first executive director and, even before that, had senior strategic and tactical responsibilities in the embryonic movement.

Shaw recalls that, toward the end of the Winnipeg meeting, an electrifying moment occurred. Many of the delegates were heading for the doors, preparing to fly home after a significant and, in some ways, exhausting event. One of the wrap-up speeches was just beginning. The speaker was Harper, then just twenty-eight and wrestling with the daunting dual role of Reform policy development and university economics studies.

The voice was clear. The sentences were short, compelling, and delivered with a cool passion. Shaw says that people began turning around in their tracks and heading back to their seats to listen. That was the moment Shaw began to take serious note of Harper.

In *The New Canada* (1992), Preston Manning offers an account of the Winnipeg Assembly:

The best speech and most influential presentation at

the founding assembly . . . was given by Stephen Harper, on the subject of "Achieving Economic Justice.". . .

Harper's address to the Winnipeg Assembly was more germane to western concerns and more detailed in its analysis and its policy prescriptions than any speech by any cabinet minister to a western audience since the Conservatives [had come to power in 1984].

At the same time, Harper's delivery was eloquent and understandable to those not well-versed in economics, marking him as a potential spokesman, candidate and member of parliament. People who had been told that the Reform Party consists of well-meaning simpletons mouthing naïve solutions to complex problems should study Harper's speeches on behalf of Reform.

Harper began by introducing the topic of justice and injustice, fairness and unfairness, in the economic treatment of western Canada within confederation. He buttressed his argument that confederation had failed to provide economic and constitutional equality across the country with figures on job creation funds, Supply and Services procurement, CBC programming, civil service employment, federal government offices, federal expenditure/taxation balances and regional allocations of federal development grants, and federal government policy priorities.

He then went on to argue that applying fairness criteria to national decision-making structures and processes required such things as more effective regional representation in national institutions; regional impact assessments of major federal policy initiatives by Treasury Board; the removal of inter-provincial as well as international barriers to trade; reform of the welfare state to balance taxpayer's interests with client interests and to focus social spending on those with the greatest needs, special-interest lobby groups, including political parties. He ended with a direct and stirring appeal for westerners and Reformers to become "the essential element of a new political majority that will promote fairness for all Canadians."

Harper's address shattered all the stereotypes (reactionary backward-looking, narrow, simplistic, extreme) that are often applied to a new political party struggling for legitimacy from a western base. It combined youthful enthusiasm and idealism with wisdom, breadth of vision and practical solutions to real problems. It was greeted with a prolonged standing ovation . . . and I knew that the party had found a potential policy chief.

Then, on April 5, 1991, six months before Frank Atkins signed off on "The Political Business Cycle and Fiscal Policy in Canada," Harper made another significant speech at the Reform's Saskatoon Assembly. Entitled "A Reform Vision of Canada," that discourse symbolically marked both his own political coming of age and his party's emergence as a truly national force.

Let's read Manning's analysis of that speech in *The New Canada*:

Stephen reported and reflected on the feedback that

the Reform party had received on constitutional issues from its own members as well as other sources. In his judgment, a majority of Canadians in large parts of the country "do not want the constitutional status quo. . . . [They] do not want special status for Quebec or a special deal for Quebec. . . . [They] do not want to establish a highly decentralized confederation (as proposed in the Quebec Liberals' Allaire Report). . . . Canadians do not want a constitution built around the ideology of the Left or the Right. . . . [And they] do not want top-down executive federalism."

What do Canadians want in terms of a new constitutional order? "Reformers," said Stephen, "want a strong country built by those who want in, not by those who want out." At this point he was interrupted by such strong applause that it took several minutes to restore order.

Continuing on the affirmative side (what Reformers want, rather than what Reformers oppose), he declared that "Reformers want a genuinely federal system, including a strong national government with strong regional representation and strong provinces to protect cultural identity and regional character. . . .

Reformers want a constitutional division of powers designed to fulfill the needs that Canadians share, including the need for a competitive economy, a responsible community, a sustainable environment. [And] Reformers want a country that respects the democratic values that Canadians share. . . ."

Stephen then concluded by asking the delegates to answer, by their votes on policy and strategic resolutions over the next three days, three tough questions that the media and the public would insist we answer before the next federal election: "First, we will be asked whether the Reform Party is committed to its vision of Canada. Second, we will be asked whether the Reform Party's agenda is free from extremism, especially on issues like language and immigration. Third, we will be asked whether the Reform Party is a positive and united political movement."

In the audience for that speech was Laureen Teskey, who later became Harper's wife and the mother of his two children, Benjamin and Rachel. The speech — and the speaker — thoroughly impressed her. A computer graphics professional who ran her own business, she was already involved in Reform work, including production of the *Reformer* quarterly newspaper and other party printed materials. The work took her to the Saskatoon Assembly, where her closer relationship with Harper began.

But Saskatoon also symbolized the emergence of Reform as a national force. One of the major items of business was passage of a motion whose major thrust was to permit Reform to establish constituency associations and nominate candidates in ridings east of the Manitoba-Ontario border. The motion, low key and softly worded as it was, nevertheless created high drama for the assembly.

Until then, Reform had been viewed, in both the west and the east, as a western protest or reform movement. Indeed, some of the original proposal papers written by Manning had given the embryonic party the working name of Western Reform Party. And one of its most popular slogans was "The West wants in!"

The National Energy Program instigated by Pierre Trudeau and never fixed by Brian Mulroney to the satisfaction of many westerners, helped to fuel the fires of western discontent. And Manitobans were unhappy that the 1986 servicing contract for 136 CF-18 jet fighters went to Montreal's Canadair, rather than Winnipeg's Bristol Aviation, even though the latter had a lower bid and a higher technical competence rating.

Those two issues gave that slogan feet and provided Reform with the traction it needed to build in the four western provinces. There were signs, however, that many Ontario people were looking westward for a political alternative. So the Saskatoon Assembly became the decision-making place on that issue. Among the several hundred Ontario observers at the assembly, dozens were wearing white T-shirts emblazoned with the Reform logo and the slogan "The East wants in!"

When the expansion motion passed — overwhelmingly, it should be noted — the delegates and observers broke into a lusty singing of "O Canada." Cliff Fryers, the Calgary lawyer who was, at the time, Reform president, restored calm and promptly told the crowd, tongue firmly in cheek, "You realize, of course, that you are all out of order."

These Reform assemblies helped to give Harper a profile with many of the people with whom he would work in the years to come. While a relatively small group of people mentored him, his circle of influence would grow of necessity as he became an increasingly public figure in the leadership of the Reform, Alliance, and Conservative Parties.

CHAPTER FOUR

Into the Political Back Corridors

Harper chose to leave the Commons only three years after being elected. Returning to Calgary, he took on the job of heading up the National Citizens Coalition, a fiscally conservative advocacy group.

Tensions between Harper and Manning have been cited as the primary reason for Harper's leaving Parliament, but both Harper and Rick Anderson, Manning's former senior advisor, maintain that whatever tension existed at that time was, for all practical purposes, put to rest when Harper defeated Stockwell Day for the leadership of the Canadian Alliance in 2002. At that time, Manning and Harper were able to clear the air both publicly and privately.

Furthermore, Anderson says that Manning was one of

Harper's political and spiritual mentors in the early Reform years — and remains so. But, as with his own father, one of the ways that Harper accepts mentorship is by ceding to the mentor the role of a "sounding board." (Anderson also points out that Manning is and has been a spiritual mentor to a fair number of his associates through the years, including himself and Diane Ablonczy.)

Harper is a voracious reader. And while he reads more in the fields of political, economic, and historical materials than in that of spiritual or theological matters, he does not neglect the latter. His brother Robert reports that much of his heavy reading in the religious area has been C. S. Lewis and Malcolm Muggeridge.

The *Ottawa Times*, a religiously and politically conservative newspaper published for several years in the 1990s, quoted Harper, in December 1995, as suggesting that his pilgrimage from religious scepticism to Christian commitment occurred during his university years. Harper told the paper that he had eventually become an adherent of the Christian and Missionary Alliance, Preston and Sandra Manning's denomination of choice since the late 1980s, when they moved from Edmonton to Calgary.

The interview, by Jonathan Bloedow, one of the newspaper's editors at the time, made the spiritual side of the interview just one aspect of the profile. It quoted Harper as suggesting that "I'm not a person who was born with a particular set of values and has held them my whole life. I like to think that the values I hold today are in the process of a life of education," both academic and experiential. "Twenty years ago [when he was sixteen], I would have been an agnostic, central Canadian liberal. And my life experiences have led me to come to other conclusions about both life and political values . . . both intellectually and spiritually."

Speaking in broader terms, Bloedow noted that "Mr. Harper . . . has comprehensive and deeply held views, but he says he deliberately carries himself in a way that is perhaps unusually mild for a political ideologue. 'My own life experiences have led me to have, I think, a fairly well-developed political philosophy, but also to develop it in a way where I can understand and make it a point to understand the other points of view.'"

Some of Harper's early thinking about Quebec come out in the profile.

> He says his deep concern over the Quebec issue really came to a head since beginning his involvement with Reform, although he says he has always had an interest in Quebec, an interest which actually led him to learn French as a boy. "I went through the shift of wanting to save the country at all costs to wanting to keep the country together in a way that was positive and governable and not necessarily at all costs — and to recognize that there are limits to what can be done to deal with Quebec nationalism."

Keep in mind that Harper was making these statements shortly after the 1995 Sovereignty Referendum. At the time, he was involved with Manning in drafting what eventually was adapted by Jean Chrétien and shaped into the Clarity Act.

> On a certain level [Quebec nationalism] can only succeed or fail; it can't really be compromised.

"People who think that Quebec should form an independent state believe it as an axiom. They're not going to change their view, or at least [not] through a process of constitutional concession. . . ."

He also points out what he considers to be a dangerous feature of the Quebec secession debate. He says both sides in Quebec descended into "sort of anti-democratic practices or McCarthyism" by "basically saying you must adopt a wide range of public policy issues, whether it's on the constitution or on the welfare state or whatever, and if you don't adopt these views, then you're breaking up the country. . . ."

Obviously, Harper's spiritual development, which parallelled his emerging political interest, has been critical in his understanding and handling of the religiously based social conservatives. Harper has taken seriously the task of bringing them constructively into the mainstream of the new Conservative party, to the occasional chagrin of the Red Tories, who would sooner their "colleagues" hive off and join the Christian Heritage Party.

Always viewed as a policy wonk, even more so than Manning, Harper has, through the years, pulled together a team of confidants seemingly designed to keep him anchored to Conservative principles but strategic enough to make the principles understandable to potential political supporters.

For Harper, the emphasis was on the former; for Manning, it was on the latter. Manning would speak of the populist need to keep the people — the "grassroots" — fully informed so they could provide intelligent feedback to the policy process. He saw referendums and recalls as significant factors in making conservative populism work. And, in managing his MPs after he was elected to the House of Commons and was leading the Reform Party there, Manning developed a four-step set of guidelines for working with constituents on issues, particularly those that had social policy implications. I will briefly state that four-step process.

1. The MP should state his or her views on a particular issue. If, for example, the issue is abortion, the first step is the member's opportunity to make clear his or her views about abortion.

2. The member should then arrange a forum in which he or she can get an accurate reading as to whether there is constituency consensus on the particular issue. If the issue is abortion, the member is expected to use the opportunity to interact with the people on the issue, both listening to and challenging his or her constituents.

3. If there is a consensus — if, for example, it appears that ninety percent of the constituents are somewhere on the anti-abortion/pro-life side of the spectrum, the member is encouraged to vote according to the wishes of his or her constituents.

4. If constituents are clearly split on the issue, the member is expected to vote according to his or her own conscience in the absence of a clear party policy on the issue.

For Harper and Tom Flanagan, with whom he worked in the Reform policy office in Calgary in the early days of the party, the emphasis was on framing policy and political principles in detail, thus providing leadership to the people.

And for Harper, at least, the difference between him and Manning on the populism question was a generational one. When Harper was emerging into the political process, polling was becoming increasingly scientific. Thus, it was becoming possible to get a reading on what the population was thinking by asking good questions of a sufficiently random sample. One might call this "high-tech populism."

Harper was — and remains — comfortable with this approach. As far as he is concerned, it saves a lot of time that could be used for thinking through policy and process in a calm and reflective manner. For Manning, however, the scientific approach was not a fully satisfying substitute for actually interacting with people in their places of living, working, and recreating.

In those early days of Reform, I had a window on that process but did not really recognize the policy/populism tensions percolating at Reform headquarters. I was in Vancouver, spending about twenty-five hours a month editing the *Reformer* newspaper in 1990–91. (I resigned the contract in early 1992, telling Manning that I wanted to be free of direct political entanglements in case a later opportunity came to write something significant about Canadian politics. That opportunity emerged in 1996 after the death of Ernest Manning. The result was *Like Father, Like Son*.)

During my *Reformer* editing tenure, I often received policy statements of from two thousand to three thousand words from Harper or Flanagan. They were lucidly written, professionally prepared, and reflected the depth of thought characteristic of both men.

But they were too long, I believed, to keep the attention of the average newspaper reader. As a journalist, I maintained that even the most policy-aware Reformer would develop glazed-over eyes after the third or fourth paragraph of a long policy statement. Furthermore, as a journalist trained in community newspapering, I wanted to ensure a high "unit count." That meant I wanted several different stories on each page, covering a wide range of subjects of interest to the eclectic group of readers in the Reform community.

Before I shuffled off the *Reformer* scene, we worked out a pretty fair arrangement. I would write some short stories about emerging policy forums and statements. Then elsewhere in the newspaper, sometimes in a policy insert or supplement, the full statements appeared. In fact, in the run-up to the 1991 Saskatoon Assembly, the inserts that appeared in the *Reformer* helped to frame the work done in the constituencies in preparation for the assembly policy discussions and votes.

I had little direct contact with either Harper or Flanagan. My line of reporting was to Diane Ablonczy, who had been the first president of Reform and, during my *Reformer* tenure, was communication director for the party. Occasionally, Manning would stop by my Vancouver office, if he was in town, to read page proofs if they were ready. I was always pleased when he made very few changes to the copy, whether it was my short stories or the longer policy pieces. He explained it once, to my pleasant surprise, to a group of Vancouver party workers. "I don't know what it is," he said, in his trademark quizzical cadence. "But Lloyd seems to have a way of writing that puts it clearly."

But enough horn blowing.

In many ways, the Harper-Manning discussions were two sides of the same coin and reflected the six sides of conservatism. At the risk of oversimplification, those six sides can be described as follows.

> • **Fiscal conservatism** is the concept of conservatively motivated controls on government spending and economic intervention, with accompanying emphases on low taxation and reliance on the markets, rather than a command economy directed by the state.
>
> • **Social conservatism** emphasizes pro-life and pro-family policy positions. Pro-life positions, as popularly defined, call for protection of the right to life for the unborn and the disabled. Pro-family positions call for protection of traditional family definitions, particularly those that see the ideal family as being headed by a mother and a father.
>
> • **Democratic populism** is a concept that, in its broadest sense, calls for involvement of the "common people" in the development of policy. One historic Canadian definition of social conservatism — one that grew out of the Prairie populism of Tommy Douglas and Ernest Manning — was somewhat broader than the current pro-life/pro-family stance. It assumed respect for issues raised out of socialist and liberal mind-sets and pressed for conservative responses to those issues.
>
> • **Progressive conservatism** encourages moderate political and social change as well as economic nationalism.

The most radical of progressive conservatives are sometimes nicknamed "Red Tories." In the Canadian context, the Progressive Conservative name grew out of the 1942 election of John Bracken, then the Progressive premier of Manitoba, as the leader of the federal Conservative party. A condition of his acceptance of that leadership was that the party name be changed to Progressive Conservative. The Progressives were an agrarian-based free-trade party that peaked in the 1920s and 1930s. It elected federal MPs in Ontario and Manitoba and held provincial power in Manitoba for a number of years. The "progressive" moniker generally denoted a left-leaning approach. It was, and remains, a common self-description for socialists.

• **British Toryism** is the advocacy of the preservation of established institutions and (according to *Webster's*) "combined with political democracy and a social and economic program designed to benefit the 'common people.'" Some of the cultural differences between conservatives in eastern and western Canada grow out of the eastern propensity to draw on historic British Toryism and the western inclination toward American-style fiscal and social conservatism.

• **Libertarianism**, advocacy of the doctrine of free will, espouses absolute and unrestricted liberty, especially of thought and action.

The periodic fracturing of conservatism has generally fallen somewhere on either geographic or philosophic fault lines represented by some permutation or combination of the above six categories.

I examined two of those fault lines in June 2005 in one of my Ottawa *Watch* pieces that responded to an Anthony Westell column in the *Globe and Mail* on June 4:

> Anthony Westell has done a pretty good — but somewhat oversimplified — job of tying together the social conservatism of the late Ernest Manning, Alberta premier from 1943 to 1968, and the emergence of evangelical Christian candidates in the new Conservative Party. . . .
>
> In fact, in making the linkage, he spoils his rationale by failing to recognize two fault lines, one of which flows from the other.
>
> Ernest and Preston Manning's social conservatism grew out of Prairie populism. It was a conservative response to the social gospel aspect of Tommy Douglas's Saskatchewan socialism.
>
> A close reading of *Political Realignment: A Challenge to Canadians*, the Ernest Manning book to which Westell refers, will show that the Manning definition of social conservatism was, in effect, the recognition of the issues raised by socialism and the social gospel and the applying of conservative concepts to resolve those issues.
>
> In an August 25, 2002, interview with Joe Paraskevas, then of the *Calgary Herald*, Ray Speaker amplified on that broader social conservative (socon) definition. Such socons, he suggested, were fiscal conservatives who envisaged caring communities meeting their social needs with a minimal of state involvement. Speaker was a good person to make that point,

having been a part of the continuum as both a Social Credit and a Conservative provincial cabinet minister in Alberta, an original "Class of '93" Reform MP, and one of the "emissaries" in the Tory-Alliance merger. And, to boot, he is an evangelical Christian — like Marvin Olasky, the Texas journalist who coined the concept of compassionate conservatism.

True, the Manning socons valued the traditional Christian perspectives on life and family. But they resisted the single-issue mind-set.

That came later, when a socon subset saw fighting abortion and gay rights as a necessary ingredient in a culture war with the social left.

This brings us to examine the second fault line.

In the pulling together of the various conservative strands making up the new Conservative Party, Stephen Harper and Peter MacKay have attempted to downplay the culture wars in the interests of advancing, among other things, the political realignment advanced by the Mannings.

They have, after all, tried to learn from history.

In the late '80s, Jake Epp was the health minister in Brian Mulroney's PC cabinet. A devout Mennonite, he was one of about thirty Conservative MPs that Mulroney affectionately called his "God Squad."

Epp attempted to develop compromise abortion legislation to replace that which had been thrown out by the Supreme Court of Canada.

For his efforts, he was attacked by the social left but, more ironically, by the social right, who believed that nothing short of a complete ban on abortions would do.

During the rise of Reform, this same, relatively doctrinaire form of social conservatism began to assert itself in the new party. Some of these socons were former Progressive Conservatives who had been unhappy with Epp's abortion stance.

Preston Manning encouraged such socons to work with the Reform Party but would not permit them to take it over. And that led to the more doctrinaire among them banding together behind Stockwell Day, whom they envisaged as being more malleable than Manning.

In learning from history, Harper appears to have grasped the necessity of dampening the culture wars and getting socons to bring their values to the larger conservative table. He — and MacKay — are counting on the viability of the "big tent."

Westell implies that the recent nomination of several evangelical Christian Conservative candidates must be causing Preston Manning to smile.

That is not necessarily so. Manning will not be happy if such candidates are active participants in an internecine culture war.

He is probably happy about the nomination of Darrel Reid, who was once his chief of staff. Yes, Reid was president of Focus on the Family Canada, a Christian pro-family advocacy group, for several years. But he is more than that. He earned his history Ph.D. at Queen's under the watchful eye of the late George Rawlyk, an ordained Baptist who once wrote press releases for Tommy Douglas.

So Reid is a "big tent" socon who should, in fact, make both Preston Manning and Brian Mulroney happy — not to mention Stephen Harper and Peter MacKay.

Much of what Harper attempted in assuming leadership of first the Canadian Alliance and then the Conservative Party of Canada took into account the need for a clear understanding of conservatism's several facets. He also had to shape strategies to permit those facets to rub together, to resonate, to create enough critical mass to establish a viable government-in-waiting.

In Chapter Seven, "Rebuilding Consensus," we will examine some of the strategies and tactics that Harper used as he began to round up all the stray conservatives and encourage them to quit fighting with each other. Part of his task was to reduce the incidence of political "culture wars" and to build the framework for bringing the strengths of the various cultures into the functioning of the new party.

An understanding of Stephen Harper's increasing grasp of the intricacies of conservatism involves an examination of that amorphous group affectionately dubbed, by both admirers and critics, as the "Calgary School." We will talk about this group's influence in Chapter Eight, "The 'Hidden Agenda.'"

CHAPTER FIVE

Laureen and Lewis

When Deborah Grey credits Laureen Teskey with turning Stephen Harper into a gentler, warmer human being, she reflects a fair amount of reality. Various stories have emerged about the conditions that brought them together.

During the 1980s, when Harper was doing his undergrad work at the University of Calgary and working for Tory MP Jim Hawkes, he formed a relationship with Cynthia Williams, a journalism student. Eventually, she became his fiancée, but in due course, she mentions, they "drifted apart." As Harper left his Conservative connections behind and became involved in Reform, Williams moved on in her television career. Still single, she is an advertising writer and producer at Calgary's CITY-TV (formerly A-Channel).

Intriguingly, Williams introduced Harper to Teskey, believing that they might be well suited. A computer graphics designer by profession, she was doing contract work for Reform, so soon she began to see him around the office. In 2002, Laureen jocularly told William Johnson that she rejected the idea that, "if you want to meet a man, join a church." Rather, she suggested, joining a political party was the route to go.

Their first date, however, arranged through Calgary-Nose Hill Reform MP Diane Ablonczy, was a fundraising gala at Centre Street Church, the megacongregation where Ablonczy and her husband, Ron Sauer, worship.

Teskey was briefly married at about the same time as Harper was engaged to Cynthia Williams. That marriage was followed by a long bus trip from Cairo to Capetown for the purpose of seeing something of the world before settling in domestically. As it turned out, that bus trip served to build independent MP David Kilgour's appreciation for the Harpers when he had breakfast with them after leaving the Liberal caucus. Kilgour's heart, in many ways, is in Africa, having been the minister responsible for Latin America and Africa in Chrétien's cabinet. Kilgour was and remains a diligent watchperson with respect to Sudanese issues, and he appreciated that Laureen was one of the few Canadians whom he had met who had been in Darfur, one of the current Sudan hot spots.

As it turned out, Teskey played a role in the successful completion of Harper's master's thesis, also in 1991. As Harper wrote, "Acknowledgement is also extended to Ms. Darlene Chrapko and Ms. Laureen Teskey, who provided extraordinarily prompt and accurate assistance, as well as numerous corrections, in the preparation of this manuscript." Additionally, Laureen, with her graphic arts expertise, provided many of the graphs and charts to illustrate Harper's arguments. And, while their friendship grew during the graphics consulting sessions, it was his landmark speech at the Saskatoon Assembly, later that year, that helped the romance to blossom.

Stephen and Laureen married on December 11, 1993, in a small civil ceremony, not long after he was elected to the House of Commons. And his decision to return to Calgary three years later was related in part to family matters. Laureen was expecting Benjamin, their firstborn, and Stephen was not too happy about the long hours associated with political life.

Laureen provides a different kind of spiritual support for her husband than do many wives of political leaders who happen to be evangelical Christians. Experiences in her family background have caused her to be cautious about becoming too involved in church activity. Some of her relatives became so immersed in a high-demand Christian group that everything else — family, work, and recreation — was left subservient. Laureen's vow, apparently, was to provide some guard against whatever temptations Stephen might have to become more caught up in church life than his time or energy would permit.

Laureen is both cautious and assertive in her verbal support for her husband. During the June 2004 election campaign, she mentioned to me that Stephen was buoyed up by informal assurances from some Christian, Jewish, and Sikh supporters that he was being prayed for in their places of worship. (That she was talking to a journalist who writes mainly on the faith-politics interface might have persuaded her to throw caution to the wind in telling that tale.)

Laureen has also become well appreciated by social conservative MPs who believe they are being marginalized in an increasingly broad party. While Stephen protects the socons from being labelled as bigots by more left-leaning politicos, it is Laureen who ebulliently encourages them to be patient and let things happen incrementally when the times are right.

Stephen and Laureen's relationship is complementary, all the more so because Laureen is strong in her own right. They work together in raising Benjamin and Rachel, recognizing their particular strengths as mother and father. Stephen, it is noted often, loves being a father. He is a hockey dad for Benjamin and pits his own strong mind against Rachel's in board games in Stornoway. Laureen takes mothering seriously.

Their relationship also contributes to Stephen's substantive advocacy for the traditional definition of marriage. Stephen and Laureen's appreciation of and respect for viewpoints different from their own help him, while advocating marriage as being between a man and a woman, to support protection of "the rights of non-traditional unions so they are afforded the same benefits as married couples."

The Harpers ensure that Benjamin and Rachel attend church frequently, with at least one of them accompanying them. One Sunday I happened to attend the Harpers' Ottawa church "home," an international evangelical congregation in the east end of Ottawa. Benjamin and Rachel were very active in that particular worship service. The occasion was "Shoebox Sunday," which, to the uninitiated, is an annual event organized internationally by Samaritan's Purse (SP), a Christian relief and development organization run by Franklin Graham. Franklin is the son of Billy, the famous and now octogenarian evangelist. Every year thousands of churches throughout North America, under a program developed by SP, lead their families through a process of packing shoeboxes with gift items for pre-Christmas distribution to children in less developed countries. Benjamin and Rachel, along with a couple of dozen other youngsters, were carrying armfuls of shoeboxes from the back of the church to the altar area so that the minister could dedicate them to God before dispatching them to the Ottawa airport.

Harper looked on with some satisfaction. Conservative economist that he is, he welcomes the opportunity for international aid most when the nongovernment sector is involved. For him, Operation Shoebox is an excellent development educational tool, functioning in harmony with his idea of what Christianity is about. While the small gifts themselves might not contribute a great deal to relieving poverty in the life of one child in Afghanistan (the destination of that particular shipment), they provide linkages for the children that help them, in later life, to connect the dots between Third World poverty and First World prosperity.

The Harpers, whether they realized it or not, were following the example set by Stephen's periodic spiritual mentor, Preston Manning. As the five Manning children grew to adulthood, they received a gift from their parents: an opportunity to work for a few months in a less developed nation with a group — usually Christian — involved in relief and development work. The Mannings and the Harpers agree that faith-based responsibility rather than state coercion can be the primary motivating factor in the relief of oppression and poverty in far-flung parts of the globe.

Comparison of the churchgoing habits of the two families provides a context for their respective faith practices. The Mannings had been part of Ernest Manning's Fundamental Baptist Church, a small congregation on the north side of Edmonton that reflected the rock-solid fundamentalist values that differentiated their kind of Christianity from that of the more liberal mainstream Protestants and that of the papal Catholics who occupied the larger cathedrals and towered stone churches of the day. In the senior Manning's *National Bible Hour* radio broadcasts and the *Prophetic Voice* magazine circulated to his listeners, the King James Version of the Bible was used exclusively. Modern translations were viewed as the domain of more liberal Bible translators who, in the view of the fundamentalists, were playing down or leaving out, conveniently, those parts of the original writings that seemed to emphasize the deity of Jesus and the moral imperatives of biblical laws and prophecies. Fundamentalist Baptists also eyed with caution the Pentecostals, who encouraged a rather emotive style of worship.

As Preston and Sandra Manning's marriage matured and their five children grew up, they sought a home church that was a little more flexible and youth friendly. Their choice at the time was the Sturgeon Valley Baptist Church near their home in St. Albert, a few kilometres north of Edmonton. Sturgeon is affiliated with the North American Baptist group originally seeded by German immigrant settlers in the Edmonton area. By the time the Mannings joined Sturgeon Valley, it was a fellowship of about three hundred people drawn from a range of ethnic backgrounds.

When they moved to Calgary, as the Reform party began to grow, the Mannings became part of First Alliance Church, a sleek megachurch that draws about 2,500 worshippers in several services each weekend. And when Preston's mother and father sold their farm and moved to Calgary, they too joined First Alliance. The parents would sit in the balcony on a Sunday morning. Preston, Sandra, and their children would be down near the front.

First Alliance, even more than Sturgeon Valley, was an energetic, youth-friendly, outreaching kind of congregation. In the church-growth vernacular of recent years, it was a trendsetter in "seeker sensitivity." Its services and programs were designed to integrate, with as little pain as possible, the person or family seeking a faith that would be emotionally and spiritually satisfying and bear some relevance to whatever they were doing out in the real world the rest of the week.

At the same time, First Alliance congregants were less demonstrably emotive than the Pentecostals, with their relative emphasis on healing, speaking in tongues, and other less cerebral forms of God consciousness. And the Alliance denomination was even less connected with a new, more charismatic, movement beginning to grow that carried with it the promise that, if it was allowed to sweep the nation, it would bring with it a great spiritual and political renewal. Some of its churches went by the name of Vineyard, Victory, Christian Fellowship, or Christian Centre (or Center — some, emanating from movements south of the border, would spell it the American way).

Keep in mind that all religious movement in the Manning family was happening during the period when Harper, the United-Presbyterian-raised religious sceptic, was cutting his political eye teeth and, in due course, courting Teskey. Harper had no social background in the turbulent changes occurring in Canadian evangelicalism. His move from scepticism to faith had come through a revisiting of his own religious background with the help of the writings of C. S. Lewis and Malcolm Muggeridge.

And, as noted elsewhere, Harper benefited from the spiritual mentoring of Preston Manning and Diane Ablonczy. The latter grew up in a Baptist pastor's home and, as an adult, has been linked closely to Centre Street Church, another Calgary megachurch that draws weekend crowds of close to five thousand.

When Harper reached the point where he believed he needed regular pastoral care and at least a modicum of formal church affiliation, his choice was not First Alliance, where the Mannings attend, but a newer spinoff, Bow Valley Alliance, a group of about 1,500 people. He speaks warmly of the influence of Brent Trask, the senior minister at Bow Valley, of his intelligence and spiritual warmth and his ability to help Harper link up with others who would encourage him in his faith pilgrimage.

And here the story moves away from a comparison-and-contrast format into a what-goes-around-comes-around mode. It draws together some of the strands that make the faith-politics interface very significant in the Conservative Party and somewhat less relevant among Paul Martin's Liberals.

After Harper moved into Stornoway, he sought a similar spiritual home for his family. Big seeker-sensitive Alliance churches are harder to locate in the national capital, Catholic as it is. But there is at least a smaller replica, East

Gate Alliance, located in a heavily French, working-class area abutting the now disbanding Canadian Forces Rockcliffe, about five minutes' drive east of the opposition leader's residence. Trask quietly communicated to Harper that someone in the opposition leader's research office, Laurie Throness, might be a good person with whom to keep in touch. Throness comes from a family replete with Alliance clergy, and he himself is an elder and periodic worship pianist at East Gate. While he has been mostly absent from Ottawa for the past couple of years, chasing his doctorate at Cambridge, Throness was able to set up the link with Bill Buitenwerf, East Gate's senior pastor.

While East Gate does not attract the crowds that throng to Calgary's many suburban megachurches, it is an excellent example of one of the Alliance denomination's other emphases — the development of multilingual churches. At present, at East Gate, there are several congregations totalling about five hundred people worshipping in different languages. Besides English, the languages of worship are Filipino, Spanish, and French. (On the other side of town, Emmanuel Alliance works with about four hundred people in Cantonese, Mandarin, and English, and Chinese Alliance is similarly involved with about eight hundred people in the same languages.)

Meanwhile, back at Bow Valley, an interesting rejigging took place. Not far from the place of worship, which had become too small for the burgeoning congregation, was Country Hills Community Church, affiliated with the aforementioned North American Baptists. Country Hills had a mortgage problem spawned by overbuilding. The leaders of the two churches negotiated a merger enabling

Bow Valley to develop a two-campus plan, an increasingly popular approach to facilitating church growth.

I can say on good authority that Harper was intrigued with the news of this merger and checked out the story to see if there was anything the Conservatives might learn about merging two similar but diversely rooted cultures. And it is intriguing that this particular merger involved the two denominations that became significant in the development of the family of Preston and Sandra Manning. What goes around comes around.

One of the noteworthy trends in all these religious migrations is the fact that many politicians, Harper among them, do take their faiths seriously but stop short of being obsessed by matters religious. "Takeovers and the Customizing of Christians," an Ottawa *Watch* piece I wrote for the *Christian-Current* newspaper shortly before the June 2004 federal election, addressed this trait.

> Let's see if we can sort out what's scary and what's not about Christian political involvement.
>
> A recent Liberal "push poll" seems designed to plant fear in the hearts of voters about a possible evangelical takeover of the Conservatives.
>
> Stephen Harper responded by pointing out that Paul Martin is a devout Catholic and he, himself, a devout Protestant — and those facts should not be an election issue.
>
> [Harper] is bang on as far as he goes.
>
> But the details surrounding religion and its relationship to political tension are worth exploring, with the help of some Christian-based sociological analysis.

The new leaders of our two largest political parties are, indeed, Christians who let their faith inform their politics.

For many years, when he lived in the same neighbourhood, Martin attended at Ottawa's Blessed Sacrament Church, a parish that has grown in the past decade from about five hundred regular attenders to close to eight thousand.

Some of that growth centres on a remarkable pastor, Joe Leclair, and his close linkages to the 1998 Ottawa Billy Graham mission and the Catholic charismatic movement. Neither factor should be considered the whole reason for the growth, but they are significant.

Blessed Sacrament is a place where Martin has received considerable pastoral care. It has helped his faith inform his politics. That he says he struggles, for example, on the issues of life and family provides some evidence of the influence of his faith.

Harper, a Presbyterian by background, finds himself spiritually "at home" in Christian and Missionary Alliance congregations in Calgary and Ottawa. Those who know him attest that he listens carefully to what his pastors and some Christian mentors have to say and finds strength in his understanding of the gospel he hears. And that helps to inform his faith.

Both men could be categorized as "customizing" Christians.

In its spring 2004 issue, *Envision*, a World Vision Canada publication, analysed a recent Ipsos-Reid survey on Christianity in Canada.

The survey worked with four categories of Christians
— census, ceremonial, customizing, and committed.

For purposes of this analysis, the customizing category for evangelicals is interesting, because it
represents — at forty-six percent — the largest group-
ing of the four.

Customizing Christians attend church fairly regularly but not because they feel they need to. They
listen pretty carefully to their pastors, but they do not
necessarily take the word of those pastors as ultimate
truth.

Positively stated, they are critical thinkers. They
appreciate what the pastor has to say, but they use the
minds God gave them as well.

A pastor who is into high control might find such
church members frustrating. One who is more of a
servant leader will consider himself or herself fortu-
nate indeed to have such people in the congregation.

Customizing Catholics show up in similar propor-
tions.

Harper, from that perspective, should not be considered "scary." His faith, grounded as it is in a
thoughtful, reflective, and respectful approach to the
Christian gospel, enhances his ability and that of his
party to approach issues in both a moral and an ethical framework.

People who try to detract from Harper or Martin's
faiths are doing no justice to the political process.

Having said all that, I recognize that people with
particular faith perspectives might well see some other
faiths and their influences on the political process as

being "scary" — perhaps because they don't understand the faith "language."

Periodically, people show up on Parliament Hill to bear witness to their particular take on the gospel. Invariably, they refer to a biblical text inscribed on the Peace Tower. The full quote reads: "He shall have dominion from sea to sea, and from the river to the ends of the earth."

Such Christians take that literally and believe the day will come when Christ sets up his dominion in Canada. In their view, he will reign from the Atlantic to the Pacific and from the St. Lawrence River to the North Pole.

Such literalism can be scary to those who might have a different vision of what God is about or who figure God has little to do with it at all. The tensions created by such fears need some tempering if the gospel is to have any meaning in the body politic.

What does all this have to do with the next election campaign?

Realistically, we work with an adversarial political system. Indeed, it is the adversarialism of that system that enables the routing of corruption and the prevailing of justice and freedom. We need those checks and balances.

But Christians need to recognize as well that, in every party, there are people who let their faiths inform them. If they are wise, they will customize their faiths to work effectively in that adversarial place we call the House of Commons.

Later in the book, we will look at the new Conservatives' first policy convention in Montreal and its spillover, especially as it related to Adscam and the same-sex marriage debate. There we will be able to check Harper's pilgrimage in the faith-politics interface.

But let's talk about Ken Boessenkool first. Boessenkool is one of the "Calgary School." He has written over thirty papers that Harper has taken seriously in his quest to make fiscal conservatism a solid plank in the new Conservative Party platform. He is also known as one of the co-authors, with Harper, of what has been called the "firewall" letter. This open letter was designed to get Albertans thinking seriously about building legal and economic "firewalls" around their province to protect against what they saw as a potential new set of federal incursions on provincial autonomy.

Less known is the fact that Boessenkool, his wife, Tammy, and their four children are part of the Canadian Reformed Church, a denomination ethnically related to various Dutch-rooted Reformed groups. And they are very serious about their faith, which embraces a fairly well-defined form of Calvinism — a belief that God is sovereign in human affairs.

Ken and Tammy home-school their children — a custom popular among some Reformed and evangelical Christians. Home-schooling is rooted in a slightly more radical interpretation of the concept that leads to the religiously based alternative to the public school system. To the Boessenkools and their compatriots, the responsibility for educating children belongs directly to the family. For the first few formative years, they believe, that schooling is best done at home.

Boessenkool is another of Harper's spiritual mentors. Although he is a few years younger than the Conservative leader, he is listened to at both the economic and the faith levels. Boessenkool left his position as a senior advisor to Harper shortly after the 2004 election. He returned to Calgary, where he became a vice-president of Hill & Knowlton, the growing government relations consultancy.

All of this background leads to four conclusions.

- There are sociological and structural similarities between religious groups and political parties that provide leaders in the respective institutions with opportunities to learn from each other — and, at times, to cross-pollinate.
- The spiritual mentorship provided to Harper by Preston Manning was modified and enhanced by Harper, given his postwar birth and his reading of C. S. Lewis and Malcolm Muggeridge.
- "Customizing" his faith has given Harper a bit of a leg up in understanding the faith impulses of the people whom he is leading and in helping them to use those impulses constructively rather than repressively.
- A number of the people with whom Harper has consulted on political matters have had spiritual and religious values to contribute as well. Throness and Boessenkool are just two examples.

It is not inappropriate to draw a parallel between Pierre Trudeau and Stephen Harper on the subject of spiritual motivation and development — especially since one of Harper's sounding boards, John Reynolds, has suggested that, if Harper becomes prime minister, he may be compared favourably in time to Trudeau. It was not until after his death that the public became aware of Trudeau's spiritual commitment and discipline within the framework of Catholic thought.

Harper's spiritual mentors have come from various branches of Protestantism. And Harper has chosen them because, within their particular fields, they have displayed the intellectual and academic rigour that satisfies him.

Yet I do not want to overplay his spiritual side. In going this far even, I risk embarrassing him by communicating that his mentors are Christian icons. But it is useful to include this background as a means of understanding more about some of the things Harper might consider when he listens to a sermon, goes for a walk to think through an issue alone, or engages in a vigorous discussion of issues with his colleagues.

To this end, I want to provide some perspectives on C. S. Lewis taken from the works of Canadian journalist Michael Coren and Charles Colson of Watergate fame. They will serve to briefly summarize the classic British Christian academic who so influenced Harper and many other cerebral Canadian Christians of evangelical and/or conservative religious leanings.

Coren, a Toronto columnist and broadcaster well known for his Christian-underpinned writing, wrote *The Man Who Created Narnia: The Story of C. S. Lewis* in 1994. He also has to his credit biographies of J. R. R. Tolkien and G. K. Chesterton. All three have won wide respect as credible articulators of the kind of cerebral Christian faith that tends to capture the attention of people who want their spiritual development to meet certain rigorous intellectual standards.

In beginning the chapter that describes how Lewis came to envisage and write *The Chronicles of Narnia*, Coren says that

Stephen (left) with brothers Grant (centre) and Robert, and their father, Joseph, taken one winter day in front of his childhood Leaside, Toronto, home. *(Photo courtesy of Laureen Teskey Harper)*

Stephen in his Calgary home in the '90s with his cats Cartier and Cabot. *(Photo courtesy of Laureen Teskey Harper)*

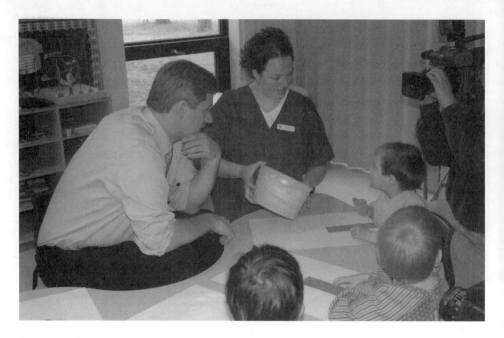

Learning the finer points of fingerpainting with young people at Pathways Health Centre for Children in Sarnia. *(© Dimitri Soudas)*

Harper often demonstrates his "concentration" look in sports photos. This one was taken at Campbell Collegiate in Regina. *(© Dimitri Soudas)*

Children Rachel (right) and Benjamin keep him company on a midway ride. (© *Dimitri Soudas*)

Stephen and Laureen register for the March, 2005, Conservative policy convention in Montreal. (© *Karine Leroux*)

Introducing Tory MPs at the Montreal convention. *(© Dimitri Soudas)*

Delivering the keynote speech at the March, 2005, Conservative policy convention in Montreal.
(© Dimitri Soudas)

Lewis once explained to a friend how certain he felt about heaven, salvation and the life to come after death. It is just through that door, he said, pointing to the door of an Oxford classroom. It's really no more complicated than that, just through the door, and it's very easy to open it and walk through. God doesn't want to shut the door, only you can do that. It was this faith in the life to come that helped Lewis through the loss of his good friend Charles Williams.

Of course, Lewis spoke of much more about life than simply the afterlife. But Coren makes the point, as do other Lewis biographers, that faith entered into consideration in many of his writings, most of which Harper permitted to seep into his own mind.

The Screwtape Letters, a compilation of imagined letters from the chief devil to those of his assistants involved in trying to undermine the faith of certain Christians, is a classic. *Mere Christianity* is considered to be one of the simplest and clearest outlines of the Christian gospel and its implications available in the English language. *Miracles* helps the rational and perhaps sceptical mind to give some credence to those aspects of the Christian faith that can be described as "supernatural." *Surprised by Joy* speaks of Lewis's emergence into a life of faith. And *Out of the Shadows* explores Lewis's re-emergence from doubt to faith following the death of Joy Davidman, the American divorcee he led to faith and later married, not long before she died of cancer.

This consideration would be incomplete without comment on political cross-pollination and realignment as parts of the environment within which Harper works. Much of the critical folklore about the religious influence in Canadian conservatism has surrounded a relatively small but vigorous evangelical subset. That segment is often portrayed as characterized by arm-waving worship, charismatic and occasionally demagogic leadership, and a belief that true democratic reform will come through a sweeping national spiritual revival that no politician save God's own anointed one will be able to control.

That was not quite Lewis's take on things, and an understanding of the religious influences within conservatism is helped by the painting of a broader picture. Pierre Elliott Trudeau and Brian Mulroney were shaped in part by Roman Catholic spiritual directors who gave guidance — not always necessarily followed to the letter — on how to live within an ethical and spiritual frame of reference. There is a parallel and equally influential framework within Protestantism that shapes the thinking of many Christians who, while respecting their more charismatic brothers and sisters, remain more trusting of a cerebral approach to faith and politics than of an emotion-based style.

A few quotations from a speech that Charles Colson of Watergate and Prison Fellowship fame delivered to the Wilberforce Forum on November 29, 1998, the occasion of the one hundredth anniversary of Lewis's birth, will provide some context for this survey. (William Wilberforce was the great nineteenth-century British evangelical Reformer whose life work was wrapped up in the abolition of the British slave trade.) Noted Colson,

> Lewis' personal influence is something of a convergence of history this particular week because

twenty-five years ago this very day — in a flood of tears in a friend's driveway in the toughest days of my life in the midst of the darkest days of Watergate — I surrendered my life to Christ. It is no accident that I am here today on the 100th anniversary of the birth of C. S. Lewis, for it was his writing that convicted me. Would I have been converted without Lewis? I am enough of a five-point Calvinist of reformed theology to believe that God had his hooks in me and would have gotten me. The Hound of Heaven, as Lewis wrote, would have pursued me, but it was Lewis whom he used to convict me.

That emotive encounter between Colson and the writings of Lewis came when Harper was still a teenager in Toronto, at least a decade before the British philosopher and other Christian intellects began impacting his own thinking. Later Colson suggests that

> C. S. Lewis did two things for me. First, he convicted me of my sin. He made me understand that I had to repent and that I could be forgiven. And he gave me an intellectual framework to understand what had happened to me in that emotional experience of surrender. I was somebody who distrusted emotion. I relied on reason. I was trained as a lawyer to think analytically. And yet I was able to understand what God had done that evening because in *Mere Christianity*, Lewis laid it out in an intellectually understandable way.

Toward the end of his speech, Colson argues that

> There is nothing more important than that we be
> "mere Christians" — it is the first line of defense as we
> enter the new millennium. What Lewis meant by this
> phrase is that while there are many differences among
> us, Catholic, Orthodox, fifty-seven varieties of
> Protestantism, we live in the same house. We discuss
> our differences, when we have them, as we emerge
> from our rooms. We do live in separate rooms because
> we understand our faith in different ways, but basi-
> cally we agree on the fundamentals of the Christian
> faith. But it is inside the house that we ought to have
> those disagreements among ourselves.

Interestingly, some of my own research on Prison Fellowship (PF), the inmate support organization that grew out of
Colson's own post-Watergate jailhouse experience, disclosed
a PF program used effectively in Colombia, where the pris-
ons were packed a few years ago with violent government
and insurgent warriors who understandably created
mayhem within the walls. The PF program was based on
concepts of Christian conflict resolution that called for deep
change from the violence-based stances to an understanding
of reconciliation. There are some indications that prisoners
released into Colombian society have been able to success-
fully practice the conciliation they learned in prison.

Lewis spent his teaching and writing years in and around
Oxford and Cambridge. He quaffed a beer regularly with
thinkers such as Tolkien, an academic colleague and author
of *Lord of the Rings*, while they talked through the philo-

sophical underpinnings of their respective Anglican and Catholic perspectives.

And, while not everyone who holds to conservatism is not Christian, or even necessarily religious, the Lewis DNA is real and to some degree pervasive. That is why those who attack Harper and his party on the ground that they are captive to right-wing religious fanaticism are somewhat off base. There is, permeating every political movement in Canada, an energizing spirituality that sometimes defies categorization. Harper has thought through that permeation. To the degree that he can utilize it as part of the alchemy that holds the Conservative Party's various cultures together, it will help to determine his success or failure in forming, in due course, the government.

Paul Martin periodically talks about a small group of evangelical pastors who meet with him in his quest to understand these people whom some in his party see as bigoted or scary. His most recent meeting with this group took place in March 2005 as the Adscam issue was waxing increasingly volatile.

The group is made up of pastors of evangelical churches whose weekend congregations run about two thousand each on average. They are called simply The Pastors' Council. The total membership is about fifty. The churches they represent come from a whole range of denominations, Anglican, Presbyterian, United, Mennonite, Baptist, Alliance, Pentecostal, and Wesleyan among them.

Their commonality is that the churches they represent all have a sociological impact on the communities they serve. So the spiritual and social insights they bring to political leaders are deemed useful enough, at least, for an occasional consultation. They have been known to meet with senior MPs of all parties in the House of Commons.

The March meeting with Martin was facilitated by John McKay, Liberal MP for Scarborough-Guildwood and parliamentary secretary to the finance minister. A lawyer who is a sophisticated social conservative, McKay is known for cofounding the Canadian branch of the Christian Legal Fellowship. He also gained a little ink for telling the prime minister to get lost when it was announced that a two-line whip would prevail on the same-sex marriage vote. (That means parliamentary secretaries, as well as cabinet ministers, were expected to vote for redefining marriage.) His protests, and those of other like-minded Liberal parliamentary secretaries, caused Martin to relent, requiring only that cabinet ministers vote with the government.

McKay, tongue in cheek, told the prime minister that the megachurch pastors whom he was to meet with were the "bigots" he had heard so much about from some of his Liberal colleagues. When the culture wars are raging, the Liberals find it easy to meet with evangelical pastors and listen to them but to hint — at the same time — that those who would encourage their people to vote Conservative are the real bigots.

One antidote to the culture war, however, is the political realignment concept first introduced four decades ago by Ernest Manning. And David Kilgour has undoubtedly considered whether he might "realign." Kilgour left the Conservatives over implementation of the GST back in 1990. During Chrétien's tenure, he held foreign affairs regional portfolios in the cabinet but was dumped by Martin, in part over his opposition to same-sex marriage. There were immediate indications that Kilgour might go back to the Conservatives.

He didn't and hung on to his Edmonton-Millwoods-Beaumont seat for the Liberals by only 134 votes in 2004.

Soon after the Gomery Commission lifted the short-held ban on the "explosive" Adscam testimony, Kilgour suggested that he might well cross the floor, maintaining that he was disgusted by the scandal and couldn't see himself winning re-election as a Liberal. He subsequently did leave the Liberals and voted against the government in the spring 2005 budget vote that ended in a tie-breaking vote for the Liberals cast by Speaker Peter Milliken.

Kilgour, a devout Presbyterian who is currently chair of the Parliamentary Prayer Breakfast, represented, until his departure, the evangelical leading edge in the Liberal caucus. (John Manley, former deputy prime minister and a devout Presbyterian/Anglican with an Associated Gospel background, held that distinction during Chrétien's tenure. The new title holder is parliamentary secretary John McKay.)

All of which suggests that one of Harper's tasks is to reposition the Conservatives in such a way as to reduce the "scariness" of the culture wars and thus attract Liberals who are really Conservatives. What happens with people like McKay and Kilgour will tell, in due course, whether his best chances lie with getting Liberals to cross the floor or getting 1990s Liberal voters to repark their votes with the Tories. And Harper knows that the most fertile ground for such action is in Ontario in ridings where religious conservatives (of Christian, Jewish, Muslim, Sikh, and Hindu persuasions) hold a balance of power and can be won over.

All the aforementioned lays the groundwork for exploring the evangelical legacy in the various parts of conservatism, the major burden of the next chapter.

CHAPTER SIX

The Evangelical Legacy

The stories in the previous chapter about shoe-boxes in church, customizing Christians, and so on provide a glimpse of the long-standing evangelical Christian legacy that has figured prominently in both the western-based Conservatives and the Social Credit/Reform/Canadian Alliance construct.

This legacy has been significant in pockets of the west, Ontario, and Atlantic Canada almost since Confederation. In Quebec, the countervailing influence has been Catholic. The Catholic influence tended to taper off in the 1960s during the secularizing process connected with Quebec's "Quiet Revolution." In the west, the evangelical influence grew because evangelical Christians held enough voting strength to create balances of power in many ridings. "Bible belts" in the Fraser Valley, some rural areas of the Prairies, southwestern Ontario, and Atlantic Canada have often allowed the playing out of that balance. In this chapter, I want to review that influence briefly from the beginning before outlining how Stephen Harper handles the legacy.

Most Canadian prime ministers have been Roman Catholic, usually reasonably devout, but always careful not to let it appear that their religion played too much of a role in their political activity. In fact, there have been two evangelical Christian prime ministers and a third who leaned that way: Alexander Mackenzie (Liberal, 1873–78), John Diefenbaker (Conservative, 1957–63), and Lester Pearson (Liberal, 1963–68). Both Mackenzie and Diefenbaker were robust Baptists; Pearson was the reasonably devout son of a Methodist-cum-United minister.

Kevin Kee, a McGill historian specializing in Protestant revivalism, has even written that Canada's first prime minister, Sir John A. Macdonald, known for his heavy drinking habit, converted to Christ in 1888 at a Crossley-Hunter Methodist revival meeting in Ottawa. His conversion apparently stuck and brought his imbibing pretty much under control, although there is little in the records to indicate where he stood on the religious issues of the day.

Furthermore, William Lyon Mackenzie King, Liberal prime minister most of the time in the 1920s, 1930s, and 1940s, was a devout Presbyterian, although his excursions into spiritualism set him apart a bit from orthodox Protestantism or evangelicalism.

But the legacy that has impacted most on Harper entered the federal scene about the time he was born, during the regimes of Diefenbaker and Pearson. And it began two decades before in the post-Depression Prairie provinces of Alberta and Saskatchewan. That was when William (Bible Bill) Aberhart, a high school principal who ran a Bible institute on the side, became premier of Alberta, with the twenty-seven-year-old Ernest Manning as his provincial secretary. In weekly broadcasts from the Calgary Prophetic Bible Institute, Aberhart thundered his blending of biblical fundamentalism and Social Credit monetary theories as an antidote to Depression woes and the dust bowl drought of Alberta. Aberhart reigned controversially from 1935 until his death in 1943, tilting frequently at the eastern bankers and other establishment economic and political windmills. And the established institutions struck back: the courts ruled Social Credit monetary legislation *ultra vires* from time to time, citing monetary policy to be in federal jurisdiction.

Upon Aberhart's death, Ernest Manning took over the reins of both the Alberta government and Aberhart's *National Bible Hour*, which, at its peak, had a weekly Canadian audience of 600,000. Popular comedian Jack Benny's numbers were barely comparable.

When Manning died in 1996, Quebec Premier Jean Charest — then federal Conservative leader — paid tribute to him in the House of Commons. Noting that he himself had grown up in a devout Quebec Catholic home, he confessed his great respect for the Alberta premier's Christian values and reported that he and the rest of his family had listened every Sunday afternoon to his radio broadcasts. Bear in mind that this was not long after Quebec Catholics had stopped throwing their Manning-style Baptist compatriots in jail for preaching and distributing evangelical literature.

Manning, even as a young man, exuded a *gravitas* that was in stark contrast to his predecessor's bombast. He was a fiscal conservative who stayed away from Aberhart's monetary theories. Aided by the discovery of oil, he managed Alberta's economy in such a manner that the province was delivered from near bankruptcy by the mid-twentieth century. His Social Credit (now in name only) was returned with large majorities in every election from 1944 until his last, in 1967. And, shaped by his religion, he was a pragmatic social conservative. For example, in the 1950s, he radically liberalized Alberta's tight prohibition-like liquor laws, all the while warning of the social damage that alcohol abuse could unleash on the population.

Meanwhile, next door in Saskatchewan, Baptist minister/orator Tommy Douglas led the NDP's predecessor, the CCF (Cooperative Commonwealth Federation) to provincial power in 1944. Driven by the same Prairie populism that had thrown out the old order in Alberta, his movement took a leftward tilt. And Douglas was supported by evangelical Christians in Saskatchewan in much the same way as Manning was by their Alberta counterparts. It was only after Douglas went to Ottawa to lead the CCF/union amalgam that became the New Democratic Party that Saskatchewan evangelical voters, particularly in rural communities, began to shift toward more conservative parties.

Meanwhile, in 1952, Social Credit jumped across the mountains into British Columbia, where W. A. C. Bennett ran the province under that banner for twenty years. After a short NDP stint under Dave Barrett, Bennett's son, Bill, gave the Socreds another twelve years of government, aided by its ability to virtually absorb both Liberals and Conservatives into its base.

The B.C. Socreds had much of the same evangelical fervour. Campaign and nomination meetings often began with the singing of "O God Our Help in Ages Past," and Socreds had no difficulty in continuously hammering the CCF and NDP with the "godless socialist" descriptive. (For their part, in the early W. A. C. years, the socialists spoke of the Socreds as being shot through with "Nazism and fascism.")

Federally, the NDP in the west was never able to garner quite the strength of the disparate conservative movements. Both the Progressive Conservatives and the Social Credit became major factors federally beginning in 1957, with the rise of staunch Baptist John Diefenbaker. He won the confidence of a fair number of western evangelical Christians, and that helped him form a government with an astounding 211 seats in 1958, after winning a minority government the year before.

Diefenbaker's rhetoric carried the day for that one term. But his loner approach and the organizational malaise of his administration, faithfully recorded in Peter C. Newman's *Renegade in Power*, assured his reduction to a minority government in 1962. And about that time the federal Social Credit, aided and abetted to some extent by Manning, began to grow. Robert Thompson, a missionary-educator who helped Emperor Haile Selassie in rebuilding Ethiopia's education system after World War II, assumed the leadership of the federal Socreds, taking under cover the Quebec Créditiste wing led by Réal Caouette.

Thompson, Douglas, Diefenbaker, and Pearson became the leaders of what Thompson described as the "House of

Minorities" for several years in the 1960s. All four shared an evangelical slant on Christianity that they let slip into the way they did politics and certainly helped to build an increasing interest by many western evangelical Christians to get involved politically.

Thompson's friendship with Pearson and the aloofness of Diefenbaker kept a Liberal/Socred arrangement prevailing during the times that Pearson was opposition leader and later minority prime minister. And that friendship was based on Pearson's diplomatic experience with Ethiopia and Thompson's missionary tenure there.

Often when Pearson, as prime minister, needed a troubleshooter in Africa, he would send Thompson rather than his foreign affairs minister. And the two were known to actually pray together in Pearson's office at times of political or personal crisis.

When the Quebec Socred wing split off on its own, that left Thompson in the House with a rump group of just half a dozen western MPs but with a fair amount of goodwill back home that could be drawn on as necessary. With both Diefenbaker and Pearson gone, Thompson believed that his only option was to throw in with the Conservatives under their new leader, former Nova Scotia premier Robert Stanfield. Briefly stated, that move put in place a process that, twelve years and two leadership changes later, brought Brian Mulroney's Conservatives to power in a government that lasted nine years.

The meaning of all this to the future of Stephen Harper's leadership lies in a brief analysis of the various sectors of evangelicalism. In its broadest terms, it includes seventy percent of the Canadian population. It is that percentage that responds affirmatively when pollsters ask a question framed approximately as follows: "My relationship with God is predicated on my belief in Jesus, who lived, died, and rose again." Of that seventy percent, as mentioned earlier, only about one quarter attend church regularly. These are people who, if asked their religious affiliation by census takers, would fall across the Protestant-Catholic continuum and — just as significantly — across the right-left continuum.

Many national surveys indicate as well that those in this seventy percent category are more likely to vote Conservative in western Canada and Liberal in the central and eastern regions, with a minority voting across the nation for the NDP. In Quebec, of course, the vote of the seventy percent category would likely divide along the lines of the general population between the Bloc and the Liberals.

Bringing the examination a little closer to the active evangelical subset shows that it represents about fifteen percent of the population. This percentage would include people who attend church regularly and take fairly seriously the teachings of their religious leaders. They are, however, an ethnically eclectic group. In places such as the Bible belts of the Fraser Valley in British Columbia, the Mennonite, (Dutch) Reformed, Alliance, Pentecostal, and Evangelical Free churches would be their gathering places. A few miles to the west in Vancouver, Baptist, Anglican, Presbyterian, as well as urban Mennonite, Alliance, and Pentecostal outcroppings would predominate as churches of choice. And many of the congregants in those Vancouver churches would be Chinese or other visible minority people, whereas their Fraser Valley compatriots would have eastern or northern European backgrounds.

No matter their affiliation, the churches that they attend would adhere, for the most part, to the four points of what is called the Bebbington Quadrilateral (after Professor David Bebbington of the University of Bristol, who developed the formula). Those points, loosely stated, are

- **biblicism:** the belief in the authority of the Bible for Christian faith and practice;
- **conversionism:** the belief that, when one converts to Christ, he or she is spiritually "reborn" or "born again";
- **Christocentricism:** the belief that Jesus Christ is God the Son and that his life, death, resurrection, and eventual return to Earth are central to the Christian faith; and
- **activism:** the belief that Christians should share their faith and practice it for the common good.

It is that last point that motivates many evangelical Christians to become involved politically. Some do so by getting into political parties and eventually being elected to public office. Others become involved in Christian advocacy groups and form coalitions to fight for particular causes — the sanctity of life and traditional marriage, Christian relief and development, education, and other worthy causes. It can be stated safely that Conservatives in western Canada, including those who supported the Mulroney government and later the Reform Party of Preston Manning, could count a fair number of those "Bebbington" evangelicals among them.

Now comes a fascinating movement that grew and to some extent flourished as a subset of the evangelical movement between the time that Preston Manning started the Reform Party and the time that he rejigged it into the Canadian Alliance. That subset could be described as the charismatic movement, which has its roots in Pentecostalism and maintains many similarities to that movement but is often somewhat more radical.

As the mainstream evangelicals grew more educated and cerebral, the charismatic churches filled the need for a more emotive and activist form of worship. And an element of their worship often included reference to the concept that God was going to bring a great revival to the nation and that it was going to begin in the capital, Ottawa. As they became politically involved, many of their leaders spoke of the need not simply to influence the political process, as Manning would advise, but also to try to take it over in the name of Christ.

To them, as well as to some of the more conservative Catholics, Manning was good, but Stockwell Day was better and would take them further. Day had spent most of his Sundays in Pentecostal or charismatic churches, and many of their leaders, particularly in Alberta, saw him as Canada's great political hope. Briefly put, these people were able to muster the membership sales to make Day the leader of the Canadian Alliance.

Their commitment ran the gamut. Some wanted to see Day become "God's anointed leader" for the dominion that, in biblical terms, extended "from sea to sea and from the rivers to the ends of the earth." Others were more practical. They wanted the banning of abortion, the minimalization of rights for homosexuals, and the sort of religious freedom that would permit the most public denunciation possible for anything that their leaders considered an abomination. They were assisted in their task at times by such leaders as David Mainse, founder of the Christian 100 Huntley Street television show and Crossroads Christian Communications; David Demian of Watchmen for the Nations; and Canada Family Action Coalition, led by Charles McVety, president of Canada Christian College, a Toronto school that works closely with several large black charismatic congregations.

Whether of the "anointed" or the "practical" school, the charismatics could appear intimidating, almost frightening, to the more traditional evangelicals. While they shared many political goals, the traditionals considered the charismatics' tactics to be excessive and at times bullying.

Less than two years later, after Day became leader of the Canadian Alliance, many strongly articulate Christian social conservatives would shift their votes from Day to Harper, in part because he was an evangelical Christian too — albeit more cerebral than emotive. While Harper, like Manning, refused to align himself directly with the most radical social conservatives, he promised to protect their freedoms and speak out against those who called them bigots and fanatics. In turn, he asked them to bring their values to the broader conservative table so that they could contribute to the making of a party that would draw from the strengths of its various elements — social, fiscal, libertarian, populist, British-style Tory, and progressive.

Harper even gave Day a significant role to play in broadening conservatism's base by making him Conservative foreign affairs critic. Day has been able to use that role to build relations between the Conservative Party and the conservative Jewish community by advocating a strong pro-Israel position. The advocates who assist him in that role are Charles McVety and Frank Dimant, national vice-president of B'nai B'rith, a conservative Jewish human rights group. The tradeoff is that B'nai B'rith provides social conservatives with access to the conservative Jewish community, while McVety encourages the "bonding" of Christians and Jews as an alternative to Christians proselytizing Jews.

But there was another religious factor that Harper had to face, in the form of the "social gospel," which had been at the base of Douglas's New Democratic Party and its predecessor. If the various evangelical denominations represented "the Conservatives at prayer," much the same thing could be said about the United Church — especially its more liberal social justice wing. It was like "the NDP at prayer." Keep in mind that Harper grew up attending the United Church but shifted to Presbyterianism when his family changed neighbourhoods. Then, when he moved from an inherited religion to a faith of his own, he adhered to an evangelical denomination.

During that pilgrimage, Harper gradually formed the conclusion that mainstream Protestant leaders, in their embrace of the social gospel and, more particularly, liberation theology, were becoming more Marxist and less Christian. In that sentiment, he probably found considerable agreement from Malcolm Muggeridge, who, when converted to Christianity, jumped straight across the religiopolitical spectrum from left to right.

Longtime geologist friend John Weissenberger recalls many discussions with Harper that grew out of their interest in reading the kinds of classics — both dated and contemporary — that would ground them in bringing together spiritual, political, and economic issues. Muggeridge, William Buckley, and Reinhold Niebuhr were among the thinkers they read with interest. The commonality for all three was their concurrent shift, over time, from left liberalism to conservatism and from agnosticism to some measure of religious faith. Buckley's *God and Man at Yale* was a discussion starter on that level, as was an essay by liberal-cum-conservative theologian Niebuhr, and *Seeing thro' the Eye: The Prophetic Legacy of Malcolm Muggeridge*, a biography by Canadian law professor-columnist Ian Hunter. All of these discussions, it should be noted, were taking place during the years when Harper and Weissenberger were variously studying and cutting their political backroom teeth.

My own experience with Muggeridge, brief though it was, occurred in 1974 when I was a staff writer for the *United Church Observer*. The curmudgeonly journalist was at the time involved in the production of *The Third Testament*, a television series shot in Toronto. The series combined wandering through the lands that formed the basis of the Bible with reflecting on a number of the great religious thinkers, including St. Augustine, Blaise Pascal, William Blake, Søren Kierkegaard, Fyodor Dostoyevsky, Leo Tolstoy, and Dietrich Bonhoeffer.

The interview that Muggeridge gave me was never published. It was a bit of a barn-burner in terms of his critique of the contemporary liberal church, which he believed was thoroughly apostate and corrupt. The only solution he could envisage was the sort of renewal that would strip established religious institutions of their material wealth and influence so that they could start anew. Before he died in 1990, he became a Catholic of the most conservative and pietist variety, finding solace in a little chapel around the corner from his English countryside cottage.

Harper is a formidable defender of economic conservatism and is well able to draw on the likes of Michael Novak of the American Enterprise Institute. Novak articulates a conservative Catholicism to suggest that the solutions to the repression and poverty identified by the religious left are found not in liberation theology but in a compassionately applied democratic capitalism. But Harper is very careful whom he faces off against and where on this subject.

After he won the Canadian Alliance leadership in 2002, he ran in Manning's old seat, Calgary Southwest, to get a seat in the House of Commons. The Liberals and Conservatives did not run a candidate against him, in line with frequent custom when new political leaders fend for their place in Parliament. The New Democrats are not so inclined to follow custom. So they put up Bill Phipps, a former moderator of the United Church and a longtime minister of Calgary's Scarboro United Church.

Now, Phipps was already well known for having questioned, during his tenure as moderator, whether Jesus is God. Less well known but probably more significant was the major project that he undertook, as his moderator's legacy, to create a forum for Christian socialism and liberation theology. Endemic to such a forum was the strong critiquing — indeed the near demonization — of capitalism and its sometime faith-based supporters. Phipps set up his forums across Canada over the three years of his tenure. They culminated in an event, attended by some two hundred left-leaning theological and economic academics and experts, held in a committee room in the Parliament buildings, just steps from the House of Commons chamber, toward the end of his term in 1999.

When Phipps ran against Harper for the Calgary Southwest seat, he challenged the new CA leader to a debate on social justice issues. Harper bluntly declined, and in terms of political strategy he had every reason to do so. Candidates who are considered the front runners in any election contest are usually advised not to get into a debate in which the challenger might gain the upper hand.

Harper probably had good advice. Having read his 1997 Winnipeg Assembly speech on economic justice, however, as well as having familiarized myself with the arguments of both the left-wing social justice positions and the more conservative viewpoints of economic justice advocates, I would have liked to see the two go head to head.

Jeffrey Simpson, in a May 7, 2002, column in the *Globe and Mail* suggested that Phipps "be given his due for a kamikaze political campaign, even if Mr. Harper does not think so. [He] is an interesting man who has done many striking things in his life. When he loses next Monday (May 13, 2002), he will return to ministering at the Scarboro United Church."

A lawyer before he pledged the cloth, Phipps grew up in a Conservative family. But he was strongly influenced toward his social justice views when he worked for social activist Saul Alinsky while studying at a Chicago seminary. He holds the view that "the church should be called to minister on the streets and for the common good, so that, like the political process, it is with the people in their pain and trauma."

To those words, Harper would find little argument. He would maintain, however, that the practice of the kind of economic justice he talks about has arguably done more in recent history to relieve both oppression and poverty than anything the political left has been able to propose.

Religious liberals and evangelicals sometimes seem to be like ships passing in the night. And so do social and fiscal conservatives, libertarians, and British Tories, and whatever other mind-sets that answer to the conservative moniker.

We will wrap up this chapter by quoting from a young man who declared his intention to run for the Tory nomination for the Ottawa West–Nepean federal riding when he learned that Tory MPP John Baird, not a particularly strong friend of the pro-life and pro-family movement, was planning to run federally if an election was called in the spring of 2005. John Pacheco, a social conservative activist who organized an April 8, 2005, pro-male-female-marriage rally that drew an estimated fifteen thousand to Parliament Hill, declared his intention to run against Baird:

> After much thought, prayer, and reflection, I am officially declaring my intention to run for the nomination of the Conservative Party in the electoral district of Ottawa West–Nepean.
>
> I simply could not find peace within my soul if I declined to participate, especially knowing the circumstances and the candidates (and their positions) running in my riding. I don't understand how I can possibly win this nomination considering the odds and the time constraints against me to sign up new members, but I must follow what I believe to be God's calling. And that, in the end, is the bottom line.

As it turned out, Pacheco was encouraged by party back-roomers not to contest the nomination. But he provided a good example of a sense of direct linkage with God that conservative and evangelical Christians sometimes claim as part of their justification for seeking office. Conversely, others — both believers and nonbelievers — find that approach intimidating, because God has not shared that linkage with them. And, if that seeming linkage is strong enough to appear to sceptics to border on delusion, it presents a special challenge to a leader who sees both his faith and his politics in a more cerebral light.

CHAPTER SEVEN

Rebuilding Consensus

In a strong sense, the emergence of the new Conservative Party was a repeating of history. In the 1960s, a "House of Minorities" prevailed, with four parties — Liberal, Conservative, Social Credit, and New Democrat — sharing the power. For part of that time, the Liberals, under Lester Pearson, held tenuous power. Before that, John Diefenbaker's Conservatives were the governing party. The Social Credit Party, led by Robert Thompson, became decimated in that period when its Quebec wing split from the main party. In western Canada, vote splitting between the Socreds and the Tories was preventing either from growing a conservative base there. While he was conservative in orientation, Thompson got along better with Pearson than with Diefenbaker.

With the subsequent retirement of Pearson and Diefenbaker from the leaderships of their respective parties, the dynamics changed. Robert Stanfield, who had been a successful premier of Nova Scotia, ascended to the leadership of the Conservatives. Pierre Elliott Trudeau took over the reins of the Liberals. Thompson did not see Trudeau in the same congenial light in which he had viewed Pearson.

The upshot was that he rolled the Socred caucus into Stanfield's PCs. It was sort of a mirror image of the CA and PC Parties in 2003. The difference? In 1972, the western link was weak, while in 2003 it was strong.

Stanfield appointed Thompson his election coordinator for the 1972 vote. Thompson snatched defeat from the jaws of victory: the Liberals defeated the Tories 109 to 107. One of the seats lost for the Tories was Surrey–White Rock in British Columbia, where Thompson had run.

He retired from active politics, remaining a bit of a senior statesman, especially to the evangelical Christian voters in the west who could always be counted on to support a conservative party. He became chancellor of the evangelical Trinity Western University.

The Conservatives emerged strong — but not strong enough to head off the Trudeau juggernaut. It took two leadership changes and twelve years for the Tories to regain power. Joe Clark replaced Stanfield in 1976 and became prime minister in a short-lived minority government in 1979. It took the retirement of Trudeau and the replacement of Clark with Brian Mulroney for the Tories to win majority government in 1984.

One more element is worth mentioning: Mulroney was

able to build a Quebec wing to his party that drew, in some measure at least, from the Ralliement des créditistes, the old Quebec wing of the Social Credit, whose disintegration was hastened with the 1976 death of its colourful leader, Réal Caouette.

When the Conservative's grip on power began to decline in the early 1990s, Preston Manning's Reform Party, one of whose chief policy shapers was one Stephen Harper, received most of the blame. Not as much attention was paid to the departure from the Conservatives of Lucien Bouchard, one of Mulroney's key Quebec cabinet ministers. Bouchard went on to pull together the Bloc Québécois, which formed the official opposition in 1993.

That might be one reason why Harper is focusing some attention on Quebec. Arguably, the west can be considered to be "in the bag," and the Tories made some progress in Ontario in 2004. But so far the Bloc remains a significant block (pun intended) to the future success of both the Liberals and the Conservatives.

* * *

In chapter four, I referred to the six kinds of conservatism whose presence challenged Stephen Harper. As he took on the leadership of the merged parties, with Peter MacKay as his deputy, he had to quickly rebuild a political-cultural consensus that recognized the complexities of conservatism. With Preston Manning, Brian Mulroney, and the "emissaries" looking over their shoulders, the two men had a daunting task.

The road to consensus was and remains a meander. Harper, as a transplanted westerner, might understand it as a cattle roundup. MacKay, from Nova Scotia, could see it as finding out where the fish are. But, whatever the analogy, none can be completely perfect. And neither is the six-definition model for figuring out conservatism. When I outlined the forms of conservatism to Manning, he generally agreed, suggesting only that his preference would be to see constitutional matters well up in the mix. He sees constitutional reform as an essential part of making it possible for a conservative government to be elected more often than not in Canada.

Consider some other scenarios that tend to promote the culture wars within conservatism while blocking conciliation among its various protagonists.

> • David Orchard — writing on the Politics Canada website about "What Makes Me a Conservative?" — reports his allegiance to Edmund Burke's definition of conservatism: a disposition to preserve and an ability to improve. Orchard was, of course, the man who, unsuccessfully as it turned out, tried to get MacKay to abandon both free trade and any effort to reunite conservatives. In quoting Burke, he suggested that his encyclopedia calls conservatism "a political outlook that involves a preference for institutions and practices that have evolved historically over radical innovations and blueprints for reshaping society."
> • At the 2005 Conservative founding policy convention in Montreal, radical social conservatives, in their quest to undermine the party's left-wing influences, tried to get the convention to vote out the "equality of ridings" concept that the Progressive Conservatives had brought to the founding principles. This concept

allowed for the eastern Canadian ridings, with their relatively small Conservative memberships, to influence the party during its build-up segment. Part of the socon strategy was to kill off the party's left wing before the vice became versa.

• Fiscal conservatives don't want anything to happen that will prevent the proper functioning of a market economy. They want, come what may, to reduce the need for government fiscal interventionism.

• Libertarians want small government and maximum individual free will. They reject the Big Brother approach of either the David Orchard wannabes or what they see to be the socon restrictions on the definition of marriage.

• British-influenced Tories from central and eastern Canada, tied in as they seem to be with the elitist chattering classes, want to protect Canadians from too many Texas-based, Bush-whacking, American-style fiscal and social conservatives.

The first two scenarios were real and easily documented. The other three represent the kinds of rationale that regularly develop in conservatism's various sectors. They all have a common point: the rejection out of hand of some other form of conservatism that they believe will not fit their particular agenda.

Once the reins of leadership were in his hands, Harper began a process of rounding up the various kinds of conservatism. He kept broadening the parameters, helping leaders of the various sectors to respect each other's viewpoints with a view to finding common ground — and beating the

Liberals. If he had been known earlier in his career as a policy wonk, now he was showing his strategic and even tactical side.

At times, Harper risked losing one sector in order to gain another. The socons made the point, for example, that, even though he was an evangelical Christian, he was not "on our side" on abortion and marriage issues. Campaign Life Canada commended him for standing up for the definition of marriage as being between a man and a woman, then ripped into him for what the organization considered to be the gratuitous and unnecessary proposition that "nontraditional unions" be granted "equality" before the law.

In defending the socons, Harper urges their opponents not to call them bigots or otherwise demonize them. In declining to stand absolutely on the side of the socons, though, he knows he risks the possibility that they might bolt and join the Christian Heritage Party. But his study of the party membership and voting statistics tells him that that is unlikely to happen.

In running for the Canadian Alliance leadership in 2002, Harper gave no hint of encouraging the unification of conservatives. Diane Ablonczy and Grant Hill were both running on that platform. For his part, Harper seemed to be single-minded about rebuilding the CA. He claimed there was little point in talking to the PCs as long as Joe Clark was their leader — whereas Ablonczy made public the fact that she had actually shown Clark her unity plan. Nor was Harper interested in using the good offices of the dissidents to build bridges to the party.

It was only after MacKay had replaced Clark as PC leader that Harper gave any hint that he was interested in getting the parties together. And he used the good-humoured venue of the annual press gallery bun toss to advance the idea. Managing a flawless imitation of Manning's elongated speaking style, he suggested that the Reform Party founder had told him that "we need to be uniiiters rather than diviiiders." MacKay had a pretty good line that night as well. He apologized for the fact that he might have to leave early. "I told David Orchard that I would be in by eleven," he quipped, in an obvious reference to the agreement that Orchard had cornered him into signing to help assure him the PC leadership in May 2003.

Between that press gallery dinner and the Montreal convention, the rest became history. But Harper used a bit of rhetoric in his convention speech to reinforce his determination to make the Conservatives a "big tent" party. Consider the following lines.

> • Our caucus has genuine diversity . . . because we have learned that you do not build conservatism by driving traditional Protestants and Catholics out of our party but by adding to it new Canadians of many faiths.
> • This is the party of Jason Kenney and Jim Prentice, of Belinda Stronach and Stockwell Day, of Peter MacKay and John Reynolds, of Preston Manning and Brian Mulroney. [Of the Belinda factor, we will talk more later.]
> • As your leader, if you disagree with me on these matters [such as abortion and marriage], I will not call you stupid or label you a threat to Canadian values.
> • I care less about your views on these matters than whether you are prepared to respect the views of those who disagree with you.

Under those rules, Orchard's definition of conservatism would have fit into a "big tent" Conservative Party. But they also rule Orchard out because of his belief that his form of conservatism is exclusively valid. Like the radical socons who would rather leave the party if they cannot take it over, Orchard finds himself unable to fit into the tent because he has a mind-set that creates a "mirror image" of the socons' seeming political fundamentalism.

Indeed, Joe Clark himself once described Orchard as a "tourist" within the Progressive Conservatives. The best possible explanation for the "tourist" descriptive is that Orchard could well be the sort of person whose political ideology is anchored left rather than right, making him impervious to the possibility that anything to the right of Red Toryism might have some legitimacy.

Shortly before the Canadian Alliance and Progressive Conservative Parties voted on the merger, I wrote a column for the *ChristianCurrent* newspaper group in which I had a couple of hints for the benefit of socons and procons who wanted to get along in the new party. As it happened, Harper had become a reader of the newspaper because the ministers of the Ottawa church he attends saw to it that his family received a copy in their church mailbox each month.

I am reproducing the column here to show some of the challenges that Harper was facing in creating a party that might be broad enough to attract enough voters to form a government. Entitled "Of Abortion, Defunding, and Impaired Driving," it ran in the November 2003 issue of *ChristianCurrent* under the column logo of "Capital Views."

What do Marjory LeBreton and Garry Breitkreuz have in common?

We will get back to that in a minute. But let's talk first about how they differ.

LeBreton is a Progressive Conservative senator — with a self-described emphasis on the "progressive."

She toiled for three decades in the Parliament Hill offices of Tory leaders John Diefenbaker, Robert Stanfield, Joe Clark, and Brian Mulroney. She was Mulroney's last appointee to the upper chamber before he left the prime minister's office. Her background is rural Ontario, and her strident defence of Mulroney has, at times, made her an outspoken critic of those "new guys on the block" — the Reform and Canadian Alliance MPs who replaced her beloved party as the conservative presence in the House of Commons, in 1993.

Breitkreuz is one of those "new guys." He is the CA MP from Yorkton-Melville, Saskatchewan. He would confess to being a "social conservative" whose Baptist faith informs a fair amount of what he tries to do politically. As such, he is one of about two dozen MPs of evangelical Christian persuasion who are part of the CA caucus. And, because he was of the "Class of '93," he was one of those evangelicals who replaced an equal number of Tories similarly persuaded when they were swept from office. The wounds from that rupture are still there, although they are growing seemingly less important as the two parties try to figure out whether they have a future together.

Earlier this fall, Breitkreuz introduced the latest of

a periodic series of private members' bills related to abortion. His proposal received two hours of Commons debate, before falling by a 2-1 margin.

The thrust of his bill was that the Commons health committee initiate a study on whether abortion should be considered a nonessential medical procedure and thus subject to federal defunding.

It was about the mildest and most outreaching form of pro-life social conservatism thinkable. It represented Breitkreuz's recognition that, in letting his faith inform his political philosophy, he was in it for the long haul. It will take time to bring others, whose political philosophy differs, to his side. In this vote, he had some government backbenchers supporting him — like Mennonite Paul Steckle, who is the Liberal co-chair of the Parliamentary Pro-life Caucus. But some of his fellow CAers were not on side — like James Moore, Rahim Jaffer, and Keith Martin, who are considered the most socially "progressive" in that party.

And therein lies the potential commonality of the CA MP and the PC senator.

Some years ago, LeBreton's daughter and grandson were killed in a car crash caused by a drunk driver. LeBreton is blunt: she describes the offending driver as a "terrorist on wheels." Now she is a persistent advocate for legislation that would reduce the point of illegal impairment from .08 to .05. She believes that simple change would save many lives on the road.

Both politicians are blending pragmatism and principle to work toward their desired objectives: to legislate in a way that will save lives. In Breitkreuz's case, the lives saved would be of the unborn whose mothers will carry them to term if affordability is an issue. In LeBreton's instance, the lower legal limit would rein in more drunk drivers before they kill.

Both recognize that, if they are to win their respective days, they will need to reach out to people of influence who differ from them philosophically. The differences may relate to life-saving priorities, freedom, choice, government regulation, or any number of other issues.

And there, perhaps, they may find their common ground.

What do we know today about how Harper's new party stacked up to the ideal expressed in the column? First, we know that Breitkreuz is in the new party, and that is not surprising. His private members' bills on the abortion issue have become increasingly incremental. He has used the opportunity to "mainstream" his views without giving them up. Second, we know that LeBreton is still in the party, and that is perhaps a little more surprising. She was very hesitant at first, especially considering that, as a senator, she would have to choose whether to sit in the new party's caucus.

But at the January 2005 Conservative caucus meeting in Victoria, LeBreton was edging toward enthusiasm as she commented favourably on the end results of the merger. Furthermore, she was one of the first to speak out strongly in support of Harper's leadership after Belinda Stronach jumped to the Liberals. In case anyone thought otherwise, she wanted the Conservatives to know that Stronach's departure was the exception that proved the rule: between them, Harper and MacKay are pulling together all kinds of conservatives.

Both Harper and MacKay have been clear that bringing together the cultures of the various kinds of conservatism requires, in some cases, a change in mindset. Especially for socons, that adjustment might go something like this: where formerly it was to ban abortions outright, the new mind-set is to find ways to reduce the number of abortions, a socially laudable and constructive goal. The new mindset requires, of course, that people for whom choice is important are not targets for demonization. They, too, are encouraged to bring their libertarian conservative values to the table.

And, for pro-choicers who are at the other end of the spectrum from doctrinaire pro-lifers, there is an issue of respect as well. Abortion-on-demand advocates particularly maintain that "choice is nonnegotiable." By that, they mean that abortion — even late-term or partial birth procedures — must not be subject to any regulation. (Even famous abortionist Henry Morgentaler is opposed, on ethical grounds, to late-term abortions.)

If Harper is able to keep people such as LeBreton and Breitkreuz in the "big tent," then he will grow an increasingly strong party. In tracking the process of rebuilding consensus, four people emerge as having significant things to say about Harper's management of the process. The four are all MPs, James Rajotte, James Moore, Scott Reid, and Jim Abbott. We will focus particularly on Abbott's take on the consensus-building issue.

Abbott, one of the tallest people in the House of Commons, is one of the original Reform "Class of '93." He comes from Cranbrook, where he was a longtime businessman. His riding, Kootenay-Columbia, in southeast British Columbia, has an economy reliant on forestry and mining. It is also home to Bountiful, made famous in recent years because it is home to a fundamentalist Mormon offshoot community where polygamy abounds.

Abbott is one of Harper's sounding boards, but he is not in the perceived inner circle, like Tom Flanagan or Ted Morton. What happens, when Harper is processing policy or strategy initiatives, is a two-stage vetting. The inner circle, most of whom he knows and trusts on most issues, is canvassed, one on one or perhaps in a phone conference call. Increasingly, e-mail and MSN work to facilitate communication. Then the leader takes the issue to a larger group. There are at least one hundred, perhaps as many as two hundred, people in the group, depending on whether one is counting regular contributors or occasional invitees. Many are MPs; others are academic contacts or former associates in the private sector. Abbott is one such. He is careful not to tip too much information on the process, perhaps because its mechanics vary from issue to issue. What he will say is that the people in the group come from many backgrounds and have a whole range of views.

Harper's approach is to ask the kinds of questions that will get the various views in the group rubbing against each other. Abbott stops short of saying that Harper puts the cat among the pigeons. But he does indicate that the leader sees his role as sitting back and listening until the issue is thoroughly canvassed.

Abbott himself has some perspectives that make him a good sounding board. He is a relative by marriage to Stockwell Day, the man whom Harper succeeded in leading the Canadian Alliance. Furthermore, Abbott has a strong small-town and rural business background, and his parliamentary experience has been mainly in finance, international business, and heritage areas. He is not in the shadow cabinet at present and sees that as a bit of an advantage.

Comfortable in international settings, particularly in Asia, Abbott brings both a fiscal and a social conservative viewpoint to any discussion, but only to a point. He is prudent even when encouraged by his leader to be frank and open. That reserve comes in part because he has been dealing with diplomats in many Southeast Asian countries, where cultures are much different from that of "mainstream Canada" (but not necessarily all that different to those of immigrant families).

Abbott admits that it took him a while to really understand Harper's approach, probably because the leader would rather listen than talk when he is managing a group to get potential policy or strategy input. Abbott points out that Harper's prodigious reading schedule backgrounds the leader for asking the kinds of questions that will get answers that go beneath the surface. The end result, Abbott says, is strong, and he finds that his respect for Harper's method and integrity has grown.

Both Abbott's and Jay Hill's perspectives indicate that, as the party has grown and broadened, so Harper has widened the circle that influences him. He still keeps in touch with the Calgary School, but he takes much of the advice of his "schoolmates" and tests it with the larger group, which includes the caucus, as well as other people across the country, from both the founding parties and the five (or six) different kinds of conservatism.

Hill's view of Harper's consensus-building process is unique. Hill was one of the dissidents who left the Canadian Alliance over Stockwell Day's leadership and became part of the Democratic Reform caucus that formed a parliamentary coalition with Joe Clark's Progressive Conservatives. From the point of being accepted back into the Alliance caucus by Harper, without having to grovel, to the date in late January 2005 when he replaced the retiring John Reynolds as House leader, Hill watched the leader from close range. He notes several strategies that Harper has used in rebuilding the consensus, first after the Day leadership trauma, then in making the Alliance-Tory merger work.

Hill also points out that Harper is not a micromanager. As long as caucus or staff members are doing their jobs, he leaves them alone. Furthermore, he notes, those longtime caucus members who were not given shadow cabinet positions, when Harper put a lot of the new young faces on the Tory front bench, were positioned to take major parliamentary committee chair and vice chair posts. So their influence continued, though their profile was reduced.

Taking back the dissidents, with a definite timeline but without having to beg forgiveness of the caucus, was the first sign, in Hill's view, of the strength of Harper's leadership resolve. Hill himself was the first to leave the PC-DR coalition, in May 2002, shortly after Harper entered the House as opposition leader. There were no conditions or promises on Harper's part. But Hill soon became Conservative Question Period coordinator, a role requiring strong skills in keeping the most public part of his party's part of the operation of the House of Commons moving along, forty-five minutes each afternoon.

Interestingly, Hill was replaced in that role by Jason Kenney, one of Day's strongest supporters, believed to have been one of the MPs most reluctant to accept the unconditional return of the dissidents. Then Chuck Strahl, who had actually led the DRs and been deputy leader to Joe Clark in the DR-PC coalition, later became deputy House leader. And when Strahl became deputy speaker, Kenney moved into the deputy House leader slot. We will return to Hill's observations in a moment.

* * *

All of this is to say that Harper, having defeated Day himself in a leadership contest, nicely handled the task of keeping Day onside and helpful rather than bitter and vindictive. More than that, he needed to see that his predecessor's considerable communication and quick study skills were put to best use. These were likely his most daunting and complex tasks in the consensus-rebuilding process.

Harper accomplished much of what he needed to do on that level by appointing Day to be the opposition foreign affairs critic. And Day took to the role like a duck to water. There he has been able to use his quick study skills to frame complex diplomatic questions in a fashion that has kept his opposite number in government on his toes.

I particularly noted that skill in meetings of the Commons subcommittee on human rights, chaired in 2004 and 2005 by David Kilgour, the former junior minister successively for Latin America/Africa and Asia and the Pacific. Kilgour, who sat four terms as a Conservative and an equal number as a Liberal, was a diplomat of the first order and, to boot, a human rights aficionado.

Also on the committee was Ed Broadbent, the former NDP leader who had come back to elective politics in his seventies after, among other things, a six-year stint as founding president of the International Centre of Human Rights. Now, Broadbent, whatever one might say about his lack of conservative credentials, is a well-educated and carefully spoken person. His undergrad degree from the University of Toronto is in philosophy, his master's is from the London School of Economics, and his Ph.D. from the U of T is in political science.

In contrast, Day has a couple of semesters beyond high school from the University of Victoria. That is not to disparage Day but to note that, with his ability to grasp the gist of an issue quickly, and Broadbent's considerable depth of understanding, the two men complemented each other, and Kilgour was there to draw out the best of both.

I sat in on two sessions on the human rights subcommittee, one hearing witnesses testify about allegations of human rights abuses in specific African countries and the other on the persecution of certain religious groups by people of other religions. In both cases, Day listened to the witnesses, then summarized what they had to say in an instant motion calling for action by the Commons foreign affairs committee, to which the subcommittee reported. When Day was done speaking, Broadbent immediately proposed several "friendly amendments" designed to flesh out and properly word Day's quickly prepared motion. Then Day congenially approved the amendments, and they were adopted by the subcommittee without further ado. The consensus building handled by Kilgour at the subcommittee level has been a godsend for Day in fulfilling Harper's expectations for him in the relatively high-profile foreign affairs shadow cabinet portfolio.

* * *

It is sometimes interesting to observe the seating arrange-ments in the House of Commons and do a little semi-educated speculation about how those arrangements, particularly on the opposition side, serve Harper's consen-sus-building agenda. I received a clue one evening when the press gallery members were invited to a Christmas reception at Stornoway, the opposition leader's residence, where Stephen, Laureen, Benjamin, and Rachel live.

This was shortly after Larry Spencer, a Southern Baptist minister, had been elected in 2000 as the Alliance MP from Regina-Lumsden–Lake Centre. Now, Spencer is a very good preacher and has strong instincts for pastoral care. And he received his theological education in the American south, where strongly held opinions about homosexuality are often more colourfully and forcefully delivered than is the case in Canada — particularly in Ottawa.

One morning, shortly before Alliance-Tory merger plans were announced, the front pages of several CanWest news-papers featured a story by Peter O'Neil in which Spencer agreed that he would not be opposed to the recriminaliza-tion of homosexual behaviour. As it happened, Spencer was the Alliance family issues critic at the time. In short order, Harper stripped him of his critic's role. Spencer, in turn, vol-untarily resigned from the Alliance caucus.

I later told O'Neil that I respected his journalistic integrity and honesty, but suggested that, given my readership, I might have handled the story a little differently, emphasizing the conundrum in Spencer's views on recriminalization.

That conundrum, to be specific, was that while he favoured recriminalization of homosexuality, he did not want gays to go to jail. And he was prepared to have a "live and let live" rapport with gay MP Scott Brison, if they both ended up being Conservative MPs in the soon-to-be-merged parties.

The point of the story is that, during the press gallery's evening at Stornoway, one of the reporters asked Harper what he would have done if he was the leader of a party with both Spencer and Brison in the caucus. The tongue-in-cheek reply was "I would have made them seatmates!" Harper was never faced with that reality, of course. Brison was well on his way to fleeing to the Liberals by the time the Alliance chief was reincarnated as Conservative leader.

* * *

An aside to that story is worth noting. A number of the socon insiders identified O'Neil as "the enemy." As a journalist — and a Christian — I could not buy that, because O'Neil had handled the interview in a most ethical manner.

Later I learned some facts that helped me to conclude that the "enemy" charge was not really justified. O'Neil attends a thriving Anglican church which is in most respects, evangelical. (I will not name the church, for I don't want to turn it into a tourist trap.) The rector of the church, as it happens, teaches periodically in a couple of Canadian evangelical seminaries.

From where I sit, O'Neil is not an adversary of Christians or certain kinds of conservatives, but is in a position to be an honest broker in the political marketplace.

How much the pastoral care he receives influences his practice of journalism is a personal question. But the socons who targeted him as an enemy could do well to review their stance, in the interests of seeing themselves as others see them.

* * *

The Spencer story led me to observe some interesting instances of seatmating on Harper's watch. Stockwell Day was teamed up with Belinda Stronach. At the time, she was the most socially liberal Conservative, and Day is the best-known social conservative. But both had internationally oriented shadow portfolios — he foreign affairs and she international trade. And they had complementary skills. Day is a smooth speaker and, as indicated earlier, a quick study on issues. Stronach is more wooden in her spoken presentations but, until she crossed the floor, was building a good reputation as a team builder.

Now, sitting beside each other in the Commons is not a time-consuming matter. It involves, on most days, forty-five minutes during Question Period. But it is a situation in which some of the best use of time is to talk to each other.

The best evidence I had was that Harper, rather than being threatened by Stronach's team-building skills, was making full use of them. Furthermore, because he does not micromanage, he left it to Stronach to do her own team building in the greater interests of caucus development. I will note two instances.

First, in the process of researching this book, I attended the Conservative winter caucus in January 2005 in Victoria. On the last day of the caucus meeting, I had to meet a 5 a.m. shuttle bus outside the hotel. Checking in at the hotel lobby, I saw Stronach in one of the alcoves punching in a number on her cell phone. For the next ten minutes, she spoke to what turned out to be her two children, in Newmarket, where it was 8 a.m. and they were just heading out the door for school. Her side of the conversation demonstrated that she was both a strong and an intelligent mother. Everything she said to her children was designed to let them know that they were important, as were the school projects in which they, with other young students, were involved.

Second, one afternoon shortly after the Montreal Conservative policy convention, I was in a Parliament buildings corridor with Maurice Vellacott, one of the stronger socons in the Conservative caucus. Stronach came by, and Vellacott left our conversation for a moment to talk with her. Their chat was about an international trade workshop at the convention in which she'd had a lead role and he a supportive one. He commented that the initiative had gone well; she affirmed him, letting him know that his work was well appreciated. Both her words and her body posture spoke of team building.

Of course, her skills in this area were first recognized when she became a pivotal figure in encouraging the Alliance-Tory merger. Yet many socons saw her as the enemy because her views on marriage (she is twice divorced and, at the time, was an "item" with Peter MacKay) and same-sex marriage (she is okay with same-sex marriage, while MacKay is not). But teamwork helps to make the five (or six) different kinds of conservatism work relatively smoothly together. That point was not lost on Harper. (Having taken a snapshot of team building when Stronach was still on the team, I should note that, in chapter thirteen, I comment on the postjump "Belinda factor.")

In commenting on how this team-building approach

works, House Leader Jay Hill lays to rest the idea that Harper relies on a secretive small group for his advice on public policy. Yes, he allows, the "Calgary School" exists and has been media-touted as his chief advice group. But Hill says that Harper processes policy, strategy, and anything else to do with running the party through not one but at least a few small groups, larger groups (of which the caucus is one of the most important), opposition research, independent research, and wide reading. And Harper listens. He also asks questions. He may or may not give hints, when questions are asked, about whether he will take the advice given.

But that advice shows up in the strategies that Harper puts forward. The Conservative same-sex marriage stance was an excellent example. He heard his caucus and other advisors saying two things. One was that most Canadians want marriage defined as being between a man and a woman. The other was that some of those wanting the traditional definition were also okay with the legitimizing of "nontraditional unions," while others were strongly opposed to such legitimization.

There are a couple of other seatmate pairings to note. First, after Deborah Grey returned from the DR caucus to sit with the Alliance, the Alliance leader had her paired with Maurice Vellacott, who had been one of Day's stronger supporters in his runs against both Manning and Harper. Second, Harper has paired himself with his deputy leader, Peter MacKay. That setup follows tradition more than being a "you guys get talking" strategy. The deputy leader always sits next to, or close to, the leader in most parties. But in many ways, it sets an example.

Depending on whom you talk to, Harper and MacKay

either are barely civil to each other or are very good friends. I am inclined to lean to the latter view, especially since MacKay's breakup with Stronach. In fact, both before and after the breakup, Harper and his wife, Laureen, modelled a traditional family to MacKay.

Chuck Strahl, now deputy speaker, had a largely unheralded informal role in ploughing the ground that led to Harper and MacKay working together. When Strahl was a dissident, and deputy leader of the PC-DR caucus, he and MacKay built a good informal rapport — one that thrived either because of or despite Joe Clark, depending on whom one speaks to. One factor was that Strahl lives on the west side of the continent, while MacKay resides on the east.

Strahl never really believed that MacKay was interested in the Tories and Alliance getting together. And he thought he had proof when MacKay signed what seemed like an anti-merger pact with David Orchard in order to secure Orchard's support on the last ballot that won him the Progressive Conservative leadership. But, as it turned out, MacKay left the door open a crack. When he signed the pact, he crossed out the sentence that Orchard proposed that banned "talks" with the Alliance, leaving in only the reference to a merger itself.

So Strahl was able to take some satisfaction that the dissidents' role was not in vain. He could say, in retrospect, that he had planted the seed. While Clark never would have agreed to a merger, MacKay eventually did.

And now Strahl is deputy speaker, the first opposition member to have been appointed thus in thirty years. The appointment gives him a leg up in becoming speaker should the Conservatives form the government. In that role, he will have access to the tools that will enable him to do politics in a way that will lead to the reconciliation of conflicting interests. (Shortly before this book went to press, Strahl wrote a widely circulated column about his new fight with cancer. He is now, with his wife Deb, making decisions concerning his political future.)

But before we leave MacKay, let's observe something about the MacKay dustup at the Montreal Conservative policy convention. A small group of socons there, wanting to minimize the influence that MacKay had on the party, rounded up enough votes to move an amendment to one of the founding principles of the merger from a workshop to the main plenary session. It seemed a small enough thing, but MacKay, as he himself put it, got his Irish up and did everything possible, including running a half-day blitz of media visits, to see that the amendment was defeated.

He and Harper avoided talking to each other directly about the issue, probably because Harper was preparing for the biggest speech of his life to that date, to take place that evening. The leader, using John Reynolds as his spokesperson, said he would, as would MacKay, vote against the amendment, favouring retention of the founding principle.

Without going into eye-glazing detail, I will just mention that the amendment would have led to departure from the "equality of the ridings" concept that gave small-membership riding associations (mostly in Quebec and Atlantic Canada) the right to send just as many delegates to a party convention as larger ones (mostly in the west). For the socons, who wanted delegate numbers to be tied to riding memberships, the issue was the opportunity to give western socons some ascendancy in the culture wars with the eastern procons.

For MacKay, for a few more years at least, while membership in the new party was building across the country, including in Quebec, the issue was one of helping to meld the cultures of the two founding parties.

On the personal side, while MacKay was letting his Irish temper get the best of him in his anxiety to see the plenary vote go the way he wanted, Harper was apparently seen, in his alleged annoyance with MacKay's reported antics, to be kicking a chair across a room. By the Saturday-morning closing plenary, with the amendment defeated, peace seemed to be restored. And, at all the right times, both Harper and MacKay had mouthed the right things to encourage party unity.

So reporters were waiting to see what things would be like with the seatmates the following Monday at Question Period. MacKay and Harper were indeed seated together. Conversation seemed slow until Harper finished asking his first set of questions. Then it became fairly animated and seemingly friendly. Whatever was bygone was, apparently, past.

Later that day, answering questions about the dustup on Don Newman's CBC show *Politics*, Harper reiterated that the case was closed. MacKay, in fact, had taken Harper's son, Benjamin, to a press-politician hockey game that Harper had to miss because of other commitments. Anyone with conflicts between kids and other appointments knows that the arrangement of a stand-in — given the concurrence of the child — shows a lot of trust. And it is that kind of trust that Harper sees growing out of his particular approach to consensus rebuilding.

Let's talk about independent research and wide reading and their influences on the consensus-rebuilding process. And here Preston Manning enters the mix again.

While many of his detractors kept raising the spectre of the Reform/Alliance founder trying to sneak his way back into elective politics, Manning talked first of all about scouting, looking for political innovation and "thinking big." At one point, the sceptics had Manning getting set to enter the Senate. (It was not a bad idea at the time, actually. But Paul Martin was not likely to let that happen.)

Ted Byfield, founding publisher of *Alberta Report*, speculated that Manning was doing work in Ontario so that he could reinvent himself as a central Canadian leader, thus appealing to those who rejected him because he was from the west. And some, such as Ezra Levant, publisher of *AR*'s de facto successor, *Western Standard*, figured that he would take a run at succeeding Ralph Klein as premier of Alberta — returning to the Manning family the post that his father had held for twenty-five years.

But close observers of Manning's actual work noted that his main assignments were educational-oriented research. Most of that work was with the Fraser Institute, the Canada West Foundation, as well as the Calgary, Toronto, and Trinity Western universities. (Trinity Western provided him with an opportunity to implement his interest in the politics-faith interface.)

Then, early in 2005, Manning placed the building blocks for the development of a Centre for Building Canadian Democracy. The centre gives feet to his contention that the chances of electing conservative governments in Canada would be enhanced by a range of coalescent activities. They would include think-tanks, research bodies, educational institutions, investment networks, communications channels, interest groups, political forums, and campaign teams.

A conservative party could benefit from such an infra-structure. And Manning, backed by many people who believe that he still has a fair amount to offer to Canada, hopes to be involved at the heart of this activity for the next decade at least. (Come to think of it, this does seem a little more suited to Manning than sitting around in an unre-formed Senate.) So Harper, and any successive Conservative leader, would have this resource available.

But part of what has made Harper tick in terms of build-ing political consensus has been his reliance not only on living mentors and associates but also on a voracious reading habit. Longtime friend John Weissenberger recalls that, when Harper started work on his master's thesis, he asked one of his professors which classic economic texts he could read in his spare time. The professor apparently replied, "I'll let you in on a secret, Stephen. No one really reads that stuff." But Weissenberger swears on a stack of textbooks that Harper did read the classics anyway. His master's thesis seems to bear out the contention. Its bibliography runs for ten pages, plus another two pages of data and sources.

And, of course, I have referred before to the fact that the cerebral part of his spiritual development is not limited to light devotional reading and sermon tasting. It takes in the densely written and worldly wise prognostications of the late Anglican philosopher-scholar C. S. Lewis (recall *The Chronicles of Narnia* and *Mere Christianity*) and Malcolm Muggeridge, the agnostic journalist who in late life converted to a generic evangelical Christianity and then to Catholicism.

All of which brings us to the revealing of the "Hidden Agenda," often touted by Harper's non-Conservative critics.

CHAPTER EIGHT

The "Hidden Agenda"

The 2004 election strategy for the Liberals included the persistent claim that Stephen Harper had a "hidden agenda" consisting of many "un-Canadian values." Because Harper was leading a conservative party, with its philosophic and policy anchor firmly in the right side of the political spectrum, the secret agenda strategy proved fairly effective. That effectiveness came not in smoking out the agenda all that well but in creating some fear in the minds of voters that the Conservatives were likely to erupt Canada into a hotbed of demagoguery, separatism, police statism, or even all of the above.

As rumours of a spring 2005 election unfolded, some

signs of a repeat performance emerged and, just as quickly, blended back into the woodwork.

The most evident "test run" of the hidden agenda strategy occurred on April 13. During Question Period that day, Prime Minister Martin attempted to deflect a question from Harper about whether he had lunched and talked contracts with a key Adscam figure. That possibility had been presented at the Gomery Commission a few days before. Rather than answer the question, Martin quickly took the unusual step for a prime minister — that of posing a line of aggressive questions to Harper.

Martin's ammunition had arrived just an hour before Question Period and from two blocks down the street, in the Westin Hotel. There Preston Manning and Mike Harris had just launched the results of a year-long research project that they had tackled under the auspices of the Fraser Institute, the Vancouver-based conservative think-tank. Manning, Reform Party founder, and Harris, Conservative premier of Ontario from 1995 to 2002, are both Fraser Institute senior fellows. Entitled *A Canada Strong and Free*, the seventy-page book presented policy possibilities in the health care, environmental, and educational fields. In Question Period, Martin glommed onto the health care reference and parlayed it into the proposition that Harper had secretly ordered the Manning-Harris study and that it was being released at that moment as Conservative Party campaign fodder.

Harper distanced himself from the charge, and the furor had died down by the next day, after both media and Liberal sources postulated that "secret agenda" tactics would not work a second time for the Liberals. Harper showed his increasing adeptness at creating distance between himself and such notions. A quick analysis of his statement and the general reportage of it is instructive.

Most news stories coming out of a speech that Harper made to a Fraser Institute luncheon in Calgary on April 29, 2005, emphasized that the Conservative leader labelled the Manning-Harris health care proposal "a non-starter." Now, two important principles in the practice of journalism are tight writing and the identification of conflict. And, in thus reporting Harper's comments, the reporters were adhering to those principles. But complete reportage on his statement is helpful in the analysis of where Harper was coming from and what leadership he needed to provide in order to bring the Conservatives toward a health care policy that would capture the attention of voters and create a viable, long-term alternative to what the Liberals had been practising. So here are several paragraphs from that speech to provide context for his "distancing" effort.

> Today, I will say some things some of you in the Fraser Institute may not want to hear.
>
> Over the years, few organizations in Canada have been more associated with putting forward bold and innovative policy ideas than the Fraser Institute.
>
> As an elected official, just as before I was elected, I have always appreciated the work that think-tanks like Fraser do in our society.
>
> But, to be fully effective, even a think-tank must be cognizant of political reality.
>
> If the Fraser Institute is looking for a party that will listen to its ideas, they have that in the Conservative Party.

After the reassuring introduction, Harper introduces his "but . . ."

> But the leader of the Conservative Party must also listen to other voices and other perspectives.
>
> Recently, two remarkable and distinguished Canadians, Mike Harris and Preston Manning, co-authored a report for the Fraser Institute on improving Canada's economy and social policy.
>
> Their analysis of Canada's sluggish economic growth and productivity was important.
>
> For example, they called for restraining the growth of government spending and cutting the tax burden on Canadian families in order to liberate our economy.
>
> The example of Ireland, which has doubled its GDP in the past 20 years through a combination of tax cuts and targeted investment — a period in which Canadian growth has remained mostly stagnant — is compelling.
>
> The authors have also attempted to give a frank diagnosis of the challenges of our health care.
>
> . . . As their prescription, the authors recommended replacing the Canada Health Act and virtually eliminating any federal role in health care.

More reassurance. Manning and Harris are given full credit for their analysis, but . . .

> With all the respect that I do have for this Institute and these men, I could not imagine a proposal that is more of a non-starter than that.

It was this sentence, of course, that got the attention of the journalists. It represented the conflict that every good story needs — the issue that separates one side from another. And that word was "non-starter." Left to its own devices, it seems to suggest that Harper is repudiating his previous health care stance in order to deflect Paul Martin's broadside.

> The Conservative Party of Canada fully supports the evolution of the Canadian health care system within the framework of the Canada Health Act.
> This is not an imposition on the provinces. The provinces themselves have agreed, in a series of accords, to respect the principles of the Act and to work within the bounds of a universal public health insurance system.
> In fact, in this province, the Canada Health Act is itself enshrined in provincial legislation.

Telling a Fraser Institute audience that there is more to life than market norms might seem risky. But if anyone can handle the risk, it would be a politician who has grounded himself in the belief in the strengths of the market system and the disadvantages of a command economy.

> If this represents a departure from the market norms that guide much of the public policy thinking of this Institute, then so be it.
> There is a consensus across Canadian society that those norms should not dominate the provision of health care services.

The ability to pay cannot control access to necessary medical services for ordinary Canadians and it will not in a national Conservative government.

I know people here share the same concerns that we do about the deterioration of our health care system over time, and I know that legitimate concerns have spurred some of these suggestions for radical change.

I just want to put these concerns in some perspective.

Now Harper creates the context, pinpointing both the bad and the good news.

First, our health care system is not unique in being under a great deal of stress.

The ageing population in all advanced countries is part of the cause.

But so is some good news. Because of better medications, more sophisticated equipment, and improvements in professional training, health care services can do far more than ever before. But these things come with costs that are higher than ever before, if not potentially infinite.

No system — certainly not the American system — has mastered this problem.

Second, the Canada Health Act has not proven to be the barrier to all innovation that it was once thought to be.

In the past few years in particular, we have seen various provincial governments experiment with a wide variety of delivery options for publicly insured services.

In my view, the weakness of Liberal demagoguery against these innovations is the obvious reality that they have allowed them to happen.

And, of course, there is the necessary political needle, the suggestion clearly enunciated, that on the other side of the aisle is a prime minister who is arguably not quite as pure as the driven snow.

A prime minister who secures his own health care in private executive health facilities that few Canadian families can access is not the poster child for a purely state-run model.

Let me speak personally here. I will never compromise public health insurance in this country, because it is the only system that most Canadian families, including my own, have ever used.

Friends, I want to conclude by reminding you that, whatever disagreements we may have on health care, we are likely to soon embark on a battle over the direction of this country — a battle that will soon determine whether this country will be among the top-tier nations of the earth, or whether it will slip among those that chronically fail to reach their potential.

On the one side will be the Liberal-NDP alliance, representing all of the worst instincts in Canadian public policy.

On the other side will be the new Conservatives, with a moderate, mainstream, and modernizing agenda, one in which I believe your Institute can see its contribution to public policy reflected.

Harper's final sentence brought his audience back to where they needed to be in understanding how a "non-starter" could be turned into a "starter." In case anyone missed it, the means was to stay the course, so that the day would come when the Manning-Harris think-tanking would slot itself into the larger issue. And in true partisan, preelection language, Harper set the new Conservatives up on the "right side" of the argument, alliteratively presented as the "moderate, mainstream, and modernizing" alternative to the "worst instincts" of the Liberal-NDP alliance.

But apart from responding to too brief media summaries about what the Fraser Institute report had to say about health care, there was no reason, really, for Harper to either defend or attack the Manning-Harris work. As several media interviews subsequently revealed, the health care proposals in *A Canada Strong and Free* were not based on the American model — which the Liberals had consistently attacked in upholding their defence of the Canada Health Act. "Two-tier" health care, with differences in accessibility, had been repeatedly denounced by successive Liberal health ministers.

Instead, the Fraser Institute project analysed health care systems in several countries whose performances on things such as waiting lists and other accessibility measures were better than either the Canadian or the American system. Nations such as Sweden (often cited by left-leaning health economists), Japan, France, and Australia were scrutinized. And another important distinction was communicated: the recommendations coming from Manning and Harris were best described as "two-track" rather than "two-tier." The two-track idea has the pragmatically familiar ring of critical path thinking often associated with engineering practice — the maintenance of alternative "paths" to a particular objective for efficiency and accessibility purposes. That concept is seen by conservative thinkers as more friendly than the pejorative feeling of "two-tier," which communicates a hierarchy of availability, depending on the means of the people looking for access.

But the release of the Manning-Harris document was instructive to the extent of revealing that conservatives, both big *C* and small *c*, were picking up on the necessity for deep research and responsible rhetoric in the shaping of conservative public policy stances. Certainly, Manning has been advancing the need for research and conservative coalition building almost since he left the House of Commons in January 2002. He was not the only person to argue that both American and British political experience demonstrated that conservative parties faired better in the long term if they were proactive rather than reactive. And such advocates suggested that the route to proactivity was necessarily paved with well-intended research accompanied by the kind of critical mass that left no room for skimpy, shallow, or overly reactionary policies or legislative initiatives.

Manning's first post-politics book, *Think Big* (2003), was heavy on research, particularly in his analysis of the economic and fiscal policy initiatives of Paul Martin as Liberal finance minister. While the book received a fair amount of short-term publicity for Manning's "tough love" critique of Stockwell Day's rise and fall, it will be best known in the long run for its potential as a textbook on political fiscal analysis.

At the launch of *A Canada Strong and Free*, before a generally sympathetic audience of two hundred, Manning made light of the suggestion that, in advocating such research, he was "doing a commercial" for the project that he was even then in the midst of launching — the Centre for Building Democracy. Among the objectives for the new centre was the encouraging of a solid backdrop of thinking and action to make it possible for Canada to have a conservative government two out of every three — or even three out of every four — elections. Such an accomplishment, Manning noted quietly, would reverse the ratios that had existed in Canada ever since Confederation.

Harper neither accepted nor rejected what Manning and Harris were saying at that point. To do so would have been to "give legs" to Martin's accusation. The fact is that Harper's whole approach, ever since his thesis-writing days, was to let the think-tanks, universities, and advocacy groups conduct research widely and then to develop the mechanisms necessary to see that good research flowed helpfully into public policy. If there was any difference between Harper's approach and Manning's, it was that Manning was a little more inclined, because of his Prairie populist instincts, to include wider public discussions of policy issues in the mix. That sometimes has left the perception, particularly among populists and "grassroots" types, that Harper is less "democratic" than he should be.

I deal with that particular question elsewhere in this book. In the next few pages, I will try to focus on how "secret" Harper's agenda is. And the examination of the "Calgary School," as well as other research and sounding board inputs, is significant to tracing the path that Harper has trod in the development of his — and his party's — agenda. In introducing that examination, it is fun to observe who really discovered the hidden agenda when.

On June 12, 2004, just fourteen days before the federal election that saw the new Conservative Party take ninety-nine seats, *Globe and Mail* columnist John Ibbitson announced that he had found it. But it had taken him about fifteen months. It was all there, he suggested, in a speech given at a Civitas meeting in Toronto on April 25, 2003.

It took *Toronto Star* editorialists almost another year — perhaps because, as reputedly liberal journalists, they had lost the scent of the conservatives for a little longer than Ibbitson. In an April 16, 2004, editorial headlined "Harper's Agenda for Huge Change," the *Star* quoted Martin as asking Harper why he was refusing to "address his hidden agenda on health care." The *Star* intoned a response thus:

> Martin is dead wrong on a key point — there is no hidden agenda.
>
> In fact, the policy agenda that Harper and the Conservatives are pursuing is fairly well-documented — and is sweeping in what it proposes.
>
> Harper's agenda covers everything from health care to same-sex marriage, tax cuts to missile defence, Supreme Court appointments to giving even more power to provincial governments. It is, indeed, revolutionary.

After a few "on the other hand" type of paragraphs, suggesting that Harper's "problem" was his shifting, sometimes seemingly more moderate, positions, the editorial continues:

For most Canadians, the most noticeable difference between the Liberals and Tories is on health care and taxes.

On health care, [Harper] openly backs the private delivery of publicly-funded medical services. He also wants Ottawa to lessen its role in health care because it falls under provincial jurisdiction. Stripping the federal government of power is a Harper theme not only for health care but also for education, help to cities and providing assistance for low-income families. It's a policy that would weaken Ottawa's role across Canada.

In addition, he remains strongly in favour of even more tax cuts. Harper also backs closer economic ties with the United States, from harmonizing tariffs to working to set up similar environmental standards.

On other issues, Harper would weaken parliament by electing senators. He would politicize the Supreme Court by having members of parliament ratify judges. He opposes same-sex marriage.

With a touch of fearsome warning, the editorial concludes, "Harper is not lacking in vision. You may or may not like that vision or his policies, but you'll need to know them better before the next election."

The Civitas speech to which Ibbitson referred was, in many respects, a benchmark for Harper, because it was the first time he expounded to any fulsome degree some of the issues surrounding the bringing together of fiscal and social conservatives.

Civitas is a below-the-radar think-tank whose major

activity is an annual conference that brings together about two hundred people, on invitation, to consider matters of politics, economics, values, communications, security, and whatever else relates to such issues. The invitees are an eclectic bunch, but they tend toward some kind of conservatism, are usually fairly well-educated, and, for the most part, have some influence on what goes on in Canada. The speeches and forums are off the record despite the fact that, among the attenders, there are usually at least half a dozen of Canada's best-known journalists.

So it was a bit of a surprise to many when, three months after Harper, then the leader of the Canadian Alliance, delivered a speech to Civitas, entitled "Rediscovering the Right Agenda," that the text appeared in the June 2003 *Report* magazine (the short-lived successor to Ted Byfield's *Alberta Report*). It did not take long for word of the speech to travel like wildfire through the Canadian conservative community.

Harper began gently enough, pointing out that

> The Canadian Alliance wrapped up its leadership race a little over one year ago. At the time, the chattering classes told us the race was about the so-called unity issue — the question of whether we should have one 'conservative' party or two. But I asked the 100,000-plus members of our party a different question: Do we actually stand for something or don't we?

In placing the issue in historical context, Harper spoke of the need for what he termed, at the time, a "conservative coalition." He pointed out that

One option is to work within an existing political party to create a conservative "coalition." In my judgment, this option is the way to go and the best vehicle to do it is the Canadian Alliance.

I also believe that a combination of existing political parties, such as the Alliance and the PCs, could potentially be an even better vehicle. But that is not Joe Clark's opinion. It appears not to be Peter MacKay's. In fact, there is no guarantee or likelihood it will ever be the opinion of a federal PC leader. They seem to prefer to use the PC Party to build their own coalition.

Moving to the heart of his thesis, Harper asked,

What is the "conservative coalition" of ideas? Actually, conservatism and conservative parties, as we've known them over the decades, have always been coalitions. Though these coalitions are complex and continually shifting, two distinctive elements have long been identifiable. Ted Byfield labeled these factions "neo-con" and "theo-con." More commonly, they are known simply as economic conservatives and social conservatives. Properly speaking, they are called classical or enlightenment liberals and classical or Burkean conservatism.

In elaborating these factions, Harper noted,

The truth is that strong economic and social conservatives are more often than not the same people, and not without reason. Except at the extremes of libertarianism and theocracy, the philosophical fusion has become deep and widespread. Social conservatives more often than not demand that the government stop intervening in individual decisions, just as classical liberals often point to the religious roots of their focus on the individual.

As Harper moved on to some conclusions about how to make economic and social conservatism compatible, he cautioned that

> Rebalancing the conservative agenda will require careful political judgment. First, the issues must be chosen carefully. For example, the social conservative issues we choose should not be denominational, but should unite social conservatives of different denominations and even different faiths. It also helps when social conservative concerns overlap those of people with a more libertarian orientation.
>
> Second, we must realize that real gains are inevitably incremental. This, in my experience, is harder for social conservatives than for economic conservatives. The explicitly moral orientation of social conservatives makes it difficult for many to accept the incremental approach. Yet, in democratic politics, any other approach will certainly fail. We should never accept the standard of just being "better than the Liberals" — people who advocate that standard seldom achieve it — but conservatives should be satisfied if the agenda is moving in the right direction, even if slowly.
>
> Third, rebalancing means there will be changes to

the composition of the conservative coalition. We may not have all the same people we have had in the past. The new liberal corporatist agenda will appeal to some in the business community. We may lose some old "conservatives," Red Tories like the David Orchards or the Joe Clarks.

This is not all bad. A more coherent coalition can take strong positions it wouldn't otherwise be able to take. . . . Many traditional Liberal voters, especially those from key ethnic and immigrant communities, will be attracted to a party with strong traditional views of values and family. This is similar to the phenomenon of the "Reagan Democrats" in the United States, who were so important in the development of that conservative coalition.

In the 2005 context, Harper's ability to look ahead was uncannily borne out, although he was not, of course, correct in every respect. True, both Clark and Orchard did not enter the coalition and in fact worked, to a greater or lesser extent, against it. But MacKay did join it. Conversely, there are businesspeople who might have been loosely linked with conservative parties in the past who like the Liberals' corporatist agenda. Minister of Industry David Emerson is one such. And there are some social conservatives who seem to accept incrementalism only in the interim. They are influenced, on the one hand, by the moral certitude of their positions and, on the other, in some cases, by the belief that a sweeping spiritual revival will obviate the need for Harper's coalition building. Their stance is that God will bring in his kingdom and reduce to naught any government that bows, in any way, to secularism and compromise. The "in" phrase of such people is the warning to "beware the apostasy."

Harper makes the point — as did Manning — that such people must take their chances with the theocracy because they will be discouraged from "taking over" the Conservative Party. And he can buttress his argument by citing the "fundamentalists" on the other side, Orchard, and, to a lesser extent, Clark (who had his own coalition during his own greatest period of influence).

Orchard, particularly, adheres to only one definition of conservatism, the most progressive or "Red" form of Toryism coming out of British roots. His anti-free-trade stance is based on what he believes to be the corrupting of conservative values by American republicans. Ronald Reagan and, ironically, Margaret Thatcher are leaders to be despised in his worldview.

That, then, is a fair consideration of the benchmarking position that Harper took early on in the process of bringing together conservatism's disparate elements. But an examination of the so-called Calgary School provides some hints about how Harper moved from an easily misunderstood "hidden agenda" to one that, by the next election, arguably could be more open and available to debate and scrutiny.

The role of the Calgary School is important in understanding the ground of Harper's social, economic, and political thinking. It indicates something of the seed source, the planting of the tree, and the strengthening and spreading of its roots. But consideration of the school's role does not extend to the point of examining how large the tree has grown and how far out its branches have spread.

Geoff Norquay, the official opposition communications director appointed by Harper to replace Jim Armour after the June 2004 election, brings some perspective to the role of the Calgary School. Norquay, for the record, comes from the PC side of the merger. He worked for Peter MacKay in his run for the Progressive Conservative leadership and for Belinda Stronach in her Conservative leadership campaign. (Norquay left the post after a year for a more nuanced and less visible advisory role with Harper. But his comments still stand.)

* * *

Some critical spin had it that Armour's move was punishment for some of the communication slips during the campaign. That spin seemed to lose credence as Harper emerged from his postelection reflection, facing the task of rebranding the Conservative Party, more than ever, as the government-in-waiting.

Armour, who had been Preston Manning's communication director, was let go by Stockwell Day and returned to his old position when Harper became leader of the Canadian Alliance. Armour had always been considered a steadying influence and someone who could stake out a long-term communication strategy. So his new posting could be seen as effectively fitting that skill set.

Armour's fine hand could be seen in the emergence of Harper and his team as ready to take the reins of government. From a position where he simply had to "look prime ministerial," the leader moved to the point where he was seen as the only one who had the Liberal government's feet to the fire on Adscam. From there, he needed to be positioned not only to convince the electorate that the Liberals no longer had the moral authority to govern but also to give voters good reason to believe that the Conservatives were a strong, competent, corruption-free fresh start.

One of Armour's recruits to the public affairs task was Neil Reynolds, former editor of the *Ottawa Citizen* and later the *Vancouver Sun*. By then retired and living in the country near Kingston, Reynolds was seen as a good pick to give seasoned counsel to the "young bucks" — of both sexes — who often populate the support staffs responsible for selling leaders and parties to "the people."

Reynolds and Armour were a good match — both preachers' kids and appreciative of the kind of Christianity engendered by C. S. Lewis. The balance of the match was interesting too. Reynolds's father was a Free Methodist pastor whose theological roots would have emphasized free will and the importance of people making their own decisions. Armour's predecessors — all seven generations of them — were Presbyterian clerics. Their sermons would have leaned toward Calvinistic concepts such as God's predetermining choices and irresistible grace.

In Christian thinking, the concepts of free will and predestination are seemingly incompatible. Yet in the development of Protestantism in Canada, those conflicting concepts were frequently mediated to the end of making faith work in the real world. The formation of the United Church in 1925, drawing from both Methodist and Presbyterian traditions, was just one example of such mediation.

So what does all this have to do with the Calgary School?

* * *

When I first talked to Norquay, about interviewing him for

this book, he referred me to an article in the October 2004 *Walrus* magazine entitled "The Man behind Stephen Harper," by Marci MacDonald. Norquay cautioned me that "MacDonald has never been known to be kind to either of our parties," referring to the Tories and the Alliance. But he suggested that the piece would be helpful to any analysis of Tom Flanagan and others who have been named, from time to time, as members of the Calgary School.

The MacDonald piece began with a subhead suggesting that "the new conservative party has tasted success and wants majority rule. If Tom Flanagan and his Calgary School have their way, they'll get it without compromising their principles."

The people most often associated with the school are Flanagan, Ted Morton, Rainer Knopff, Barry Cooper, and David Bercuson. They are seen as having bonded over the years on their fishing trips together, through their teaching and research pursuits, and from their general suspicion of the more liberal academic and ideological leanings of their counterparts in eastern Canada.

Morton's and Knopff's major contributions to Harper's thinking, according to MacDonald, are in the Charter and constitutional areas — especially on the "implications for the pet peeves of social conservatives: feminism, abortion and same-sex marriage." Cooper and Bercuson, whose academic pursuits centre on military studies, focus on Confederation, Quebec, separatism, and provincial rights questions. Flanagan's emphasis on a conservative take on Aboriginal issues, and his early move from American academe to the apparently frontier-like atmosphere of oil patch–based University of Calgary, round out MacDonald's summarization of the group of five. Among the five, then, there is a fair body of thinking with respect to the libertarian, fiscal, and more cerebral sides of social conservatism. And MacDonald argues that, if they have their way, Harper will ultimately see to it that those particular kinds of right-of-centre thinking carry the day.

MacDonald builds the case that Flanagan, as Harper's former chief of staff and campaign coordinator in the 2004 election, was to blame for the fact that the Conservatives did not achieve at least minority government status. But she suggests that the Calgary School is still in there and will continue to bring its influence to bear, even as any new Harper government takes shape.

MacDonald bolsters her arguments with respect to the school's importance to Harper with a closing quotation from Ted Byfield, founder of *Alberta Report* and, in her description, "the unabashed voice of the west since the Calgary School's professors were pups." She quotes Byfield as saying of Flanagan: "I don't think he knows how to compromise. It's not in his genes. The issue now is: How do we fool the world into thinking we're moving to the left when we're not?" And she concludes, "To those who are unnerved by that prospect, Byfield offers no cheer. 'Those people who said [the Calgary School and Harper are] dangerous — they're right!' he says. 'People with ideas are dangerous. If Harper gets elected, he'll make a [expletive] change in this country.'"

But it can be fairly stated that Harper has broadened the conservative coalition by arguing effectively for incrementalism. He speaks often of the need to nuance bold statements so that they are not subjected to misunderstanding.

As one week has rolled into another since the merger, it

has been easy, working in the parliamentary press gallery, to spot those nuances and to watch Harper as he reaches out to one group and then another with the message of conservative commonality. And he has maintained an intriguing degree of integrity by listening to the various groups, letting them rub against each other, but stopping them from destroying one another. He advocates for the conservative cultures to work together rather than to wage war against each other. Any battles in the run-up to the next election were to be waged against the Liberals and even to some extent against the NDP and the Bloc.

And, most significantly, Harper had John Reynolds as his campaign co-chair. That does not mean he has rejected libertarianism and fiscal conservatism, only that he had an experienced and pragmatic conservative pulling the strings.

Norquay maintains that he could see that change coming. He comes from the Progressive Conservative side of the merger and was that party's director of research from 1981 to 1984, gradually moving to the communications side and working at rebuilding the PCs after their 1993 rout. Until the 2000 election, he believed the PCs could come back by themselves. After that, he was persuaded that it was "likely necessary for the two parties to come together."

Norquay believes that the DR-PC coalition played a critical role in paving the way for the merger — although that was not generally recognized by either party at the time. He suggests, in fact, that the accepted wisdom within the PC caucus was that, if Stockwell Day had won the Alliance leadership rather than Harper, many more Alliance MPs would have left the caucus and joined the PC-DR.

Norquay quips that he backed a winner only once in the

PC leadership contests in which he had some say. He backed Joe Clark when Brian Mulroney won in 1983, Jean Charest when Kim Campbell won in 1993, and Hugh Segal when Joe Clark won in 1998. Only when Peter MacKay came out ahead of David Orchard and Jim Prentice in 2003 was he on the right side. Following MacKay's election as PC leader, Norquay continued to be a spokesperson for the Tory perspective.

During that time, he received a phone call from Harper in which the Alliance leader indicated that Norquay may have heard rumours about possible Tory-Alliance merger talks. He says Harper told him, "I ask you not to dismiss this opportunity out of hand." Norquay recalls that he found it interesting that the hint about the merger came from "the leader of the other party, not mine."

As time passed and the merger happened, Norquay's role in the new party emerged as Harper developed confidence in the work Norquay had done. It took a few weeks for him to respond to Harper's offer to make him communications director.

Norquay has a few thoughts about what it will take to get Harper accepted by Canadians. "Stephen established he is more than intelligent enough to be prime minister. The challenge for the next while [after the 2004 election] was to enable Canadians to see his nonintellectual side — his family, the personal side, his connection to issues that are important to the voters considering him." Norquay says that voters seek a level of comfort with political leaders — and other party members — in many ways.

In the merger, that point was demonstrated in a number of seemingly nonpolitical ways. People and politicians visiting other ridings or getting into the community together —

sometimes with their spouses and children — is just one way. And when people sit down and have a drink and dinner together, even going for walks or praying together, the differences are somehow not so large.

Part of understanding the breadth of the Harper agenda comes from examining the themes of speeches and articles that he or some of his close associates have written throughout the years. I have already referred to the speech Harper delivered on April 5, 1991, at the Reform Saskatoon Assembly — the one that caught the attention of Laureen Teskey. In that speech, just a few hours after assembly delegates voted to extend Reform's organizing boundaries east of the Manitoba-Ontario border, Harper outlined a four-point Reform "vision" of Canada — having already described the "failed constitutional agendas" of the other three major parties. He was speaking, at the time, as Reform's chief policy officer.

He stated that Reformers wanted the following.

> • *A strong country built by those who want in:* "For nearly 30 years, political elites have pursued constitutional change on the premise that Canada must accommodate those who wish to divide it, in order to stay together. . . . The government of Quebec says it wants to know what the rest of Canada wants. This request must be answered."
> • *A genuinely federal system, including a strong national government with strong regional representation and strong provinces to protect cultural identity and regional character:* "There has been no better or fairer proposal advanced for this than the triple-E Senate and the principles on which it is based. The national govern-

ment must handle national issues, and must reflect the regional realities of the federation. . . . At the same time, it is the proper role of the provinces to protect those things that make them distinct."

• *A division of powers designed to fulfil the needs that Canadians share, including the need for a competitive economy, a responsible community, and a sustainable environment:* "Canada must make significant progress toward the creation of a common market among the provinces. . . . The division of powers and responsibilities between the levels of government for social policy must be disentangled. . . . To ensure a sustainable environment, any new constitutional arrangements must have explicit provisions for environmental protection and regulation. We would propose a constitutional provision to allow both levels of government to delegate appropriate powers and create ecosystem-based agencies, along the lines of the St. Lawrence Seaway Authority, to handle environmental concerns."

• *A country that respects the democratic values that Canadians share and that will protect the interests of Canadians in the current constitutional situation:* "No new constitutional deal and no new arrangement with the government of Quebec will be accepted by us but by demonstrated popular consent, either by an election or, preferably, by a constitutional referendum law requiring the popular ratification of constitutional change."

Harper's last point provided some of the base thinking that eventually resulted in the Clarity Act. That was the legislation passed in 2000, in the wake of the near loss, by the federalist side, of the 1995 Quebec Sovereignty Referendum. While it was an act passed under the watch of the Jean Chrétien Liberal government, credit for much of the bill's language is generally ceded to Harper, with Manning providing editorial oversight. As is common in government-opposition relations, governments often reject opposition legislative proposals but reintroduce them later, slightly modified and under their own imprimatur.

In the winter 1996–97 issue of *Next City*, Harper and Flanagan co-authored a piece entitled "Our Benign Dictatorship." At the time, Harper was on his hiatus from elected politics, serving as president of the National Citizens Coalition. The article began with the premise that "Canada's system of one-party-plus rule has stunted democracy." As conservatives, they made a case for "more representative government."

Some of their thinking grew out of the Winds of Change conference held in May 1996. The main conference organizers, David Frum and Ezra Levant, wanted to encourage rapprochement between Reform and the Progressive Conservatives. That time had not yet come, although it was not as far away as pessimists among the two groups might have feared.

Attempting to tie in the prevalence of Liberal government by default with the divisions among conservatives, Harper and Flanagan wrote,

> Along the Trans-Canada Highway from Calgary to Banff lies a prominent mountain called The Three Sisters. Legend has it that a [tribal chief] placed each of his three daughters on a separate peak to keep them

away from unworthy suitors. The strategy succeeded so well that the three daughters died up there. Canadian conservatism is also a family of three sisters fated to perish in isolation unless they descend from their mountain tops and embrace more realistic expectations.

Harper and Flanagan were arguing at that point for something less than the ultimate full merger in which Harper played so large a hand.

After the next federal election, Canadian conservatives may begin to encourage limited co-operation between Reform and the PCs, leading to a system of sister parties. Outside the United States and the United Kingdom, such alliances are actually the norm in the democratic world, three examples being the Christian Democratic Union (CDU) and the Christian Social Union (CSU) in Germany, the Liberal-National coalition in Australia and various centre-right alliances in France. . . .

If co-operation is ever to work, the fragments of Canadian conservatism must recognize that each represents an authentic aspect of a larger conservative philosophy. Reformers will have to realize that there is something genuinely conservative in the Tory penchant for compromise and incrementalism. Tories will have to admit that compromise, to be honourable, must be guided by underlying principles, and that Reformers are not extremists for openly advocating smaller government, free markets, traditional values, and equality before the law. And both will have to recognize that

Quebec nationalism, while not in itself a conservative movement, appeals to the kinds of voters who, in other provinces, support conservative parties.

Playing off their earlier "three sisters" scenario, the authors suggested that "whatever happens, Canada will need some kind of effective political formation on the right. Given the repeated failures of our national conservative parties, conservatives should ponder a coalition of the right. Even if all three sisters can never be brought together, a working alliance of the two Anglophone sisters would be worth having for its own sake."

Their conclusion? Having also explored a number of different voting models — such as the alternative ballot or runoff elections — in a sidebar to the article, Harper and Flanagan noted that

> Many of Canada's problems stem from a winner-take-all style of politics that allows governments in Ottawa to impose measures abhorred by large areas of the country. The political system still reverberates from shock waves from Pierre Trudeau's imposition of the National Energy Program upon the West and the Charter of Rights and Freedoms upon Quebec. Modernizing Canadian politics to make it more representative would not only be good for conservatism, it might be the key to Canada's survival as a nation.

In February 1997, shortly after settling in to his National Citizens Coalition job, Harper wrote, in the NCC's newsletter, the *Bulldog*, that

Elected officials are constrained by the need for popularity every four to five years. The average one is
consumed by the monthly opinion polls. The really
bad ones worry about the approval of every group
coming through their offices looking for a handout.
Working with you in the NCC provides me with an
opportunity to do much more — to fight for basic
conservative values of free markets and free elections,
whether fashionable at the moment or not. . . .

Much of government is built on the turning (of
the premise of hard work, careful planning, and cal-
culated risk) on its head. Activities for which
Canadians generally decline to spend money — when
the bills must be pulled out of one's own wallet —
become "essential programs" once the funds are in the
public purse. . . .

Centuries ago, misuse of public funds was
restricted to a small coterie of court flunkies and
hangers-on. Today's modern democracies, even in this
age of deficit reduction, are beset by what Nobel
Laureate Milton Friedman called the "iron triangle"
— a vast network of bureaucratic empires, special
interest lobbies, and liberal media commentators —
which heaps sycophantic laurels on any elected official willing to hand them taxpayers' dollars and
launches vindictive rhetorical darts at those who
speak on behalf of taxpayers' legitimate interests.

Five days after the June 2, 1997, federal election, Harper
and Flanagan jointly wrote a piece for the *Calgary Herald*
entitled "On the Pathway to Power." They noted that

With the Liberal, Progressive Conservative, and New Democratic parties now in agreement with separatist Bloc Québécois and Parti Québécois, that Reform represents the greatest threat to national unity, it is inevitable that Preston Manning's party — now a permanent fixture — will break out of the West. . . .

For the past 30 years, the Liberals and PCs have taken turns playing what the journalist Peter Brimelow called the "patriot game." That is, they have used the fear of separatism, first threatened by Quebec Premier Daniel Johnson in his 1965 book *Equality or Independence*, to control national politics. A succession of prime ministers from Quebec — Pierre Trudeau, Brian Mulroney, Jean Chrétien, with Jean Charest waiting in the wings — have built their careers on "saving Canada." They have had several different approaches, and they all quite sincerely claimed to be combating separatism. Nevertheless, they needed the threat of separatism to justify their political strategies. . . .

Up to this point, Reform has triumphed in the West, but not elsewhere, because the West loses the most from the patriot game. The dynamic economies of Alberta and British Columbia disproportionately bear the cost of the regional transfers that are supposed to keep Quebec and Atlantic Canada happy. Meanwhile, the West's agenda of constitutional reform is put perpetually on hold because central Canadian elites see it as a threat to their domination of the system. . . .

This equating of the Bloc — outright separatists

— with Reformers, who are loyal Canadians, makes no sense. After all, if Reform did not exist, Quebec separatism would still be an enormous threat to the country.

On August 17, 1997, as part of a CBC TV panel of journalists, doctors, and medical resource people, Harper was asked by CBC Vancouver's Gloria Macarenko what he thought of a parallel private health care system in Canada. He replied, "I think it would be a good idea. . . . We are headed in that direction anyway. We're alone among OECD [Organization for Economic Cooperation and Development] countries in deciding that we'll have a two-tier system, but our second tier will be outside the country where only the very rich and powerful can access it — and will be of absolutely no benefit to the Canadian health care system."

Responding to *Toronto Star* medical reporter Lisa Priest's contention that "there is plenty of money in Medicare to keep health care for all of us," Harper noted that

> There are three actors right now in the Medicare system in Canada: there is the federal government, provincial governments, and the private sector. The fact is that the provincial governments have spent marginally more in recent years than they have in the past. The private sector is spending much more. It is the federal government that is spending less . . . because like all governments in the country it . . . managed its financial situation badly. But, on top of that, it has no real responsibilities in the health care field. It only gives one out of every eight dollars to health care.

The only role it has taken in Medicare has been fear-mongering about a private alternative and wrapping itself in the flag. None of this has done anything to improve the quality of care for Canadians.

Whether speaking as a politician or an advocate (as he did when he worked with the NCC), Harper is formidably articulate on economic issues. His comfort with his own thinking means that he speaks bluntly and economically, so he rarely has to add emphasis to make up for a weak argument. Those political aficionados who like spell-binding, charismatic speakers behind political podiums are perhaps those whom pollsters say do not warm up to Harper.

* * *

Ken Boessenkool, introduced earlier, has been close to Harper for many years on a policy-writing level. Currently vice-president of business development for Hill & Knowlton, a public affairs consulting firm, Boessenkool has been an economic advisor to Harper, Manning, and Day. (Boessenkool helped Day to frame the "flat tax" proposal when the latter was provincial treasurer in Alberta.)

Boessenkool is also a sounding board for Harper in an area other than economics. A devout member, with his family, of a Canadian Reformed Church, Boessenkool and his wife, Tammy, home-school their four children. That situation puts him close enough to social conservatism that he can provide Harper with some useful feedback when the Conservative leader is looking for it. The CRC is a Dutch-rooted denomination that holds pretty firmly to the theology of John Calvin. The concept that God takes more than a passing interest in the lives of his people is fairly important to the Boessenkools, and the home-schooling of their children is a significant way in which they pass on that concept.

Part of the Dutch approach to Calvinism is something called sphere sovereignty, which, simply explained, accepts the idea that God is interested in human activity of various sorts — education, politics, labour, business, and so on. Calvinists further believe that there is an understandable way for Christians to define those spheres and respond to God's initiatives within them.

A number of church-spun organizations in Canada provide ways in which to make sphere sovereignty function within society's larger settings. They include the Christian Labour Association of Canada (a union), the Christian Heritage Party, and Citizens for Public Justice (a social justice advocacy group). As well, King's and Redeemer Colleges, located respectively in Edmonton and Ancaster (near Hamilton), and a network of several hundred Christian elementary and high schools across Canada, have grown out of these Dutch Calvinist communities. But this kind of religious framework encourages, rather than discourages, members to seek well-based education and to engage in political activity — and to do so with intellectual integrity.

* * *

That background introduces an article co-authored by Boessenkool and Mark Mullins, who has been an economic advisor to Quebec premier Jean Charest and former Ontario premier Mike Harris. The article appeared in the October 2000 issue of *Policy Options*, a journal published by the Institute for Research on Public Policy, which is headed by

Hugh Segal, a highly regarded Red Tory and sometime candidate for the leadership of the Progressive Conservative Party. Boessenkool and Mullins introduce their piece by suggesting that

> Much of the debate over [Canadian] Alliance fiscal policy has focused on the plan to implement a single rate of tax. But the Alliance plan is much more than a single-rate tax. It is a detailed package meant to change the priorities in Ottawa and to shift the focus away from more spending, bigger government, and minimal tax reductions. Once implemented, it will reduce the size of our federal government, begin making meaningful payments on our national mortgage and leave more money in the wallets of working families and individuals.
>
> Criticizing the Alliance for promising to implement a single-rate tax is therefore a bit like criticizing a bicycle for having a back tire. The single rate, like the back tire on a bike, is certainly an integral part of the whole package. But a back tire does not a bicycle make. . . . The package itself is a comprehensive fiscal plan meant to address the three most basic fiscal variables: debt, spending, and taxes. . . .
>
> The Alliance plan is not an American flat tax. It is not a flat tax on consumption — the approach taken by most flat-tax advocates in the United States. It is a single-rate tax on income. It does not eliminate deductions in the tax system, as most U.S. plans do.
>
> [One of the priorities] of Alliance tax policy is to stem the movement of our best and brightest to lower-

tax climates, particularly the U.S. Average and marginal tax rates on higher incomes have been rising precipitously in the past 20 years.

Returning to the bicycle analogy, Boessenkool and Mullins note that

> The Alliance believes that it is time to replace the rickety old bicycle and its Liberal training wheels with a new top-of-the-line mountain bike. Though critics continue to trash the bike for having a back tire, the Alliance will be selling an entire fiscal vehicle that . . . cuts personal and corporate taxes dramatically to move Canada's economy forward in the long-term; enhances fairness, especially for families; reduces debt; encourages national savings and investment; lightens the burden of interest payments on the public purse; and, through smart spending, trims waste, increases accountability, and boosts the productive potential of the economy, thereby raising our standard of living.

Whew! One would expect that, if Harper got hold of this piece and retooled it to be a campaign speech, he would break up long sentences into short ones and otherwise follow the KIS (Keep It Simple) rule.

Apart from that, Boessenkool, along with Flanagan, are doing some legitimate political simplification without insulting the intelligence of their highly educated readers by using some useful illustrations — such as sisters on the tops of mountains and bicycles with more than just rear wheels.

Ten months before assuming the Canadian Alliance

leadership, Harper wrote a piece for the *Calgary Sun* entitled "Bilingualism's Become a Religion: Creed Produced No Unity and Cost Plenty." Appearing on May 6, 2001, it began, "When an Alliance MP recently rose in the House of Commons to attack the administration of official bilingualism, he did more than just challenge a government policy — he committed heresy."

Harper prefaced his analysis with one of his own experiences: "My own experience goes back to the summer of 1968. Pierre Trudeau had just come to power. My parents sent me cross town to a primitive immersion course, probably more to get me out of their hair than to help construct a new federal theology. In those days, the promise was that bilingualism would lead to a new country — more united, more fair, truly bilingual. It didn't work." Citing the 1951 and 1996 census findings, that English-French bilingualism had grown from twelve to only seventeen percent, Harper suggested that "many Anglophones, especially, have pursued immersion programs and are thus encouraged to consider themselves bilingual. But with no deep economic, social, or cultural reason to master and maintain the French language, the skill simply atrophies." His point was that there is nothing wrong with not being bilingual given Canada's geographic reality.

> A unilingual Anglophone or unilingual Francophone is as much a "real Canadian" as a bilingual one. And Quebec City or Calgary "define Canada as much as Ottawa or Montreal. . . ."
>
> The Liberals, of course, believe that emphasizing Canada's "Frenchness" will encourage more loyalty to Canada among Québécois.

But as Quebec becomes more French and the rest of Canada becomes more English, it really means the Québécois identify more with Quebec than with Canada.

So there you have it. As a religion, bilingualism is the god that failed. It has led to no fairness, produced no unity, and cost Canadian taxpayers untold millions.

I guess that's what happens when you mix church and state.

Three months later, on June 20, 2001, Harper and Flanagan wrote a piece for the *National Post* entitled "Three Tips for the Canadian Alliance: Policy, Policy, and Policy." They were, of course, playing on the real estate truism that there is nothing more important than "location, location, and location." They noted that

> In 1995, Reform put out a new fiscal blueprint — the Taxpayer's Budget advocating $25 billion in spending reductions and the elimination of the federal role in health and education through the transfer of tax points to the provinces. Here was another conservative principle — decentralization. The success of Reform's downsizing and decentralizing proposals came when Finance Minister Paul Martin borrowed heavily from Reform's proposed spending reductions in early 1995. That same budget also combined federal transfers into an annual lump sum, reducing Ottawa's control over provincial social programs.

Harper and Flanagan, reflecting their sense at the time

that Stockwell Day had more of a policy grip than Preston Manning had earlier, noted regarding the 2000 election that

> The Liberals responded with cunning — stealing the tax-cut agenda and catching the process-weary Alliance off guard by calling an early election. During the election campaign, the Alliance policy messages got confused. Nonetheless, the party received 25.5 percent of the popular vote, much better than the 19 percent Reform got in 1993 and 1997, and Canada got significant tax cuts as a result of the pressure the Alliance put on the Liberals. . . .
>
> Canadians need, and deserve, more than just an alternative, more than just strategic alliances. They need an alternative grounded in conservative ideals such as smaller government, lower taxes, the equality of citizens, and the rule of law. For if all we want is the exercise of power, we might as well join the Liberals.

Once Harper became leader of the Canadian Alliance, he had a chance to be quoted extensively for a Quebec audience. On March 22, 2002, the Montreal *Gazette* ran a question-and-answer piece by Kevin Michael Grace, then a senior editor at the *Report* (*Alberta Report*'s national edition). It was entitled "Getting Back on Track: The Canadian Alliance's Newly Elected Leader, Stephen Harper, Says His Task Now Is to Turn His Party, Often Viewed as a Regional Protest Movement, into an Alternative Government." Here are a few of Grace's questions and Harper's answers.

Q. *What do you think of the idea, advocated by* The

Report *and former Alliance fundraiser Peter White, of dividing up the country: the Canadian Alliance getting the West, and the Tories getting the East?*
A. Well, it's an idea and this party has floated it before. I floated it back years ago, as far back as 1997, as something that could be looked at. But none of these things will work unless there is leadership in the Tory party willing to do that. Joe Clark's position has been 301 candidates, period, under the PC banner. That obviously rules out that as a realistic option. So my attitude is: Unless there's some serious sign these people are interested, let's just get on with getting our own alternative ready for the next election.
Q. *When you first indicated you might run for the leadership, there was a whole spate of pieces denouncing you as a provincial extremist and thus unsuitable to be a leader of a national party. What is your response?*
A. That kind of reaction generally comes from centralist extremists. Look, my record is clear: I'm not a centralist. I'm a believer in division of powers between the federal and provincial governments and in provincial autonomy in resources and other matters. But I'm an opponent of separation and certainly of unilateral separation. There is an element among liberals — big L Liberals and liberal journalists — [that] believes we should be a unitary state. I reject that notion.
Q. *During the last election, the party was thrown into turmoil by special questions. How would you prevent this from happening again?*
A. We're really talking about moral issues, right?

Q. *Sure.*

A. I was the founding policy officer of the Reform party, and I thought we had some of the right formulae there. I think that very sensitive and clearly religious-denominational moral issues should not be issues of party policy, and the leader should be careful not to make his views the central issue. I think those issues should be left to free vote in the Commons. I think they should come up at the initiation of private members, and I think we can look at the citizenry raising them in a democratic process. But I've been very clear in this campaign: I don't believe the party should have a position on abortion or that the leader should lead an agenda on abortion. I don't believe an Alliance government should sponsor legislation on abortion or a referendum on abortion. Even in a conservative party, there are going to be wide differences of opinion on a question like that.

Q. *One final question: Over the last year and a half or so, I've heard from many people who have told me something like this: "I've devoted 10 or 12 or 13 years to this party, and then Preston Manning and his people wrecked everything (with the Canadian Alliance). I now have no interest in wasting any more of my time." How are you going to get these people back?*

A. I've heard that, but actually, I believe that most of these people badly want this party to get back on track. I know they're bitter. I know they're jaded. I understand their feelings. But the fact of the matter is that there is no alternative out there for most of us who built this party, and the consequences of losing this party would be devastating. What we've got to do is turn this party into an institution. It's too often been viewed as a popular protest movement or a regional fragment or a leader-centric vehicle or a coalition thrown together for a single election. I think the way to address that is to show people that we are prepared to build a permanent professional political institution, one that they can dedicate their loyalty to on an ongoing basis.

Let's move now to F. L. (Ted) Morton, one member of the Calgary School. A devout Catholic and moderate social conservative, his specialty is in constitutional matters. A University of Calgary political science professor, Morton served a short stint as official opposition research director during Stockwell Day's tenure before becoming one of Alberta's senators-in-waiting. When the wait became seemingly endless, he decided to run provincially and became a member of the Alberta legislature in November 2004. He is viewed by some socons as a possible successor to Premier Ralph Klein.

Intriguingly, Morton is one of two close advisors to Harper who have chosen to pin their hopes on increased provincial vigour rather than remain too involved in a conservative national unity quest. The other is Ken Boessenkool. Neither has any particular axe to grind with Harper himself, and both remain in contact with the federal Conservatives and their leader. But they see Alberta and the west as the interesting places to be in the next few years.

Some clues about Morton's thinking are evident in the Fifth Annual Mel Smith Memorial Lecture that he delivered at Trinity Western University in the Fraser Valley on March 7, 2003. Entitled "Our Turn: A New Course for the West," the address suggested that "Alberta and British Columbia must begin to forge a new relationship with Ottawa. To succeed in this endeavor, we must choose reforms whose success depends on our own actions, and not those of Ottawa or other provinces."

Before quoting further from the lecture, let's look at the context as it relates to both the political influence of the late Mel Smith and the university that hosts the annual lecture in his memory. For three decades during the B.C. premierships of W. A. C. Bennett, Dave Barrett, and Bill Bennett, Smith was one of the key people who framed the constitutional positions of the West Coast province up until and including the 1982 institution of the Charter of Rights and Freedoms.

As it happened, Smith was an evangelical Christian whose mind worked well beyond the tenets of his faith but remained anchored to them in a cerebral fashion. So, when he knew that he had not long to live, he placed his archives at Trinity Western, a 3,500-student, forty-four-year-old institution that aspires to be the evangelical equivalent of Brian Mulroney's alma mater, St. Francis Xavier University in New Brunswick.

The Mel Smith lecture brings some focus each year to political and public policy values reflecting western, sometimes Christian, and/or conservative outlooks. Besides Morton, some of the lecturers in past years have been Trudeau-era MP and sometime B.C. Liberal leader Gordon Gibson, Preston Manning, and Ken Carty, a spearhead of the B.C. Citizens' Assembly. In his lecture, Morton put forward the thesis that

If Western Canadians want a secure, democratic, and prosperous future, they must plot a new path. Rather than focusing solely on increasing Western influence in Ottawa, it is time to start reducing Ottawa's influence in the West. Provincial governments have failed to use all the powers at their disposal to insulate their societies and economies from the discriminatory and costly policies imposed by Ottawa. . . .

They must rehabilitate the notwithstanding power to shield their societies from the new judicial imperialism fostered by the Charter of Rights. In short, Westerners must learn to play federal politics like Quebeckers.

Morton cited "policy losses," such as the Canadian Wheat Board "monopoly," the Kyoto Accord, and the Gun Registry, as well as a list of constitutional losses — including lack of progress on a reformed Senate — as points where the score runs against the west. Among his proposals were several challenges to what he described as "harmful federal policies":

1. Maximize provincial responsibility for health care.

2. Hold a referendum on Senate reform.

3. Initiate a legislative and constitutional challenge to the Kyoto Accord.

4. Also initiate a legislative challenge to the Canadian Wheat Board monopoly.

5. Undertake a Charter challenge to the federal Gun Registry.

6. Also undertake a constitutional challenge to the regional veto statute.

7. Consider withdrawal from voluntary milk and egg marketing boards.

On the surface, these points provide fair fodder for the Liberals when they are looking for Harper's secret agenda. While some of the Liberal rhetoric has drifted into the "yellow alert" territory on the political thermometer, one comment in the spring of 2005 provided a less emotive Liberal perspective. It came from John McKay, Liberal MP for Scarborough-Guildwood and parliamentary secretary to the finance minister.

McKay could easily be judged the Liberal who would most likely run for the Conservatives if he lived in Calgary rather than Toronto. He is a Baptist who is moderately socon, a co-founder of the Canadian Christian Legal Fellowship, and a lawyer with strong experience in working with religiously based nongovernment development agencies.

With cool reason, McKay suggested that the Liberals are the only real federalist party, that the Conservatives could more accurately be described as a "provincial rights" party. And he said that this difference could be an issue in the next election.

I dealt earlier with Harper's pivotal speech to Civitas on April 25, 2003, particularly as it related to his views on the formation of a conservative coalition. Frequently in discussions of this issue, the name of Edmund Burke is raised as a means of giving some historical and philosophical context to social values in a conservative worldview. Burke, an eighteenth-century Anglo-Irish political philosopher, was sometimes described as one of the founders of Anglo-American conservatism who highly valued social order. Harper suggested that part of the renewal of conservative influence in Canada involved not so much a radical redefinition as a shift of balance between the economic and the social sides of conservatism. He suggested that

> In particular, Canadian conservatives need to rediscover the virtues of Burkean conservatism as a key component of that balance. Rediscovering this agenda, to paraphrase Ted Byfield, means not just worrying about what the state costs but also worrying about what the state values.
>
> For example, we need to rediscover Burkean or social conservatism because a growing body of evidence points to the damage the welfare state is having on our most important institutions, particularly the family. Conservatives have to give much higher place to confronting threats posed by modern liberals to this building block of society.

Harper pointed to child porn and spanking issues as reflecting part of this struggle. And he saw Burkean philosophy as playing a role in foreign affairs debates.

> [The] emerging debates on foreign affairs should be fought on moral grounds. Current challenges in

dealing with terrorism and its sponsors, as well as the emerging debate on the goals of the United States as the sole superpower, will be well served by conservative insights on preserving historic values and moral insights on right and wrong. . . .

Conservatives must take the moral stand, with our allies, in favour of the fundamental values of society, including democracy, free enterprise, and individual freedom. This moral stand should not just give us the right to stand with our allies, but the duty to do so and the responsibility to put "hard power" behind our international commitments.

Let's return to Ken Boessenkool for a moment. In the summer/fall 2003 issue of *Inroads*, he wrote an article entitled "A Conservative Template for Welfare Reform." Stated briefly, the "template" was a focus on early intervention, making work pay for families with children and targeting workfare carefully and sparingly. He suggested that this template "has proven to be a way to reduce welfare use, poverty, and the cost to taxpayers, and increase jobs for the poor." The idea is to "both keep people off welfare in the first place and to wean those who have become dependent from the system. Strategies for preventing the onset of welfare dependency focus on welfare *applicants* rather than welfare *recipients*. Known in the parlance as 'early intervention,' this approach includes lower benefits, tighter administration, screening, and time limits."

Boessenkool offered two case studies, which he described as the "Cardinal reforms in Alberta" and the "Mike Harris reforms in Ontario." The Alberta reforms, instituted in 1993 by then Minister of Family and Social Services Mike Cardinal, operated "in conformity with conservative early intervention principles. . . . [The] number of people on welfare fell by about 35,000 (one third of the 1993 caseload in Alberta) as a result of lower intake." The Ontario results were not nearly as dramatic, Boessenkool suggested, because intervention was not early enough. He also pointed out that "the key element in the Harris government's reforms was a mandatory workfare program for employable individuals. This program has been poorly targeted, is exceedingly expensive, and has been a bureaucratic nightmare. It is a good example of the adage that 'workfare is a word some conservatives use to justify bigger government.'"

Then there was the famous "firewall" letter, an open letter to Alberta Premier Ralph Klein, published on January 24, 2001, in the *National Post* and several other Canadian papers. Signed by Harper (then president of the National Citizens Coalition), Tom Flanagan, Ted Morton, Rainer Knopff, Andrew Crooks (then chair of the Canadian Taxpayers Federation), and Ken Boessenkool, it urged repatriating certain powers to the provincial government. It began

> During and since the recent [2000] federal election, we have been among a large number of Albertans discussing the future of our province. We are not dismayed by the outcome of the election so much as by the strategy employed by the current federal government to secure its re-election. In our view, the Chrétien government undertook a series of attacks not merely designed to defeat its partisan opponents, but to marginalize Alberta and Albertans within Canada's political system.

The flashpoint triggering the letter was the feds' singling out Alberta's health care system, particularly as it was seen to be drifting beyond the ken of the Canada Health Act.

The letter proposed five actions for the Alberta government to initiate as antidotes to federal incursions — noting that all could be taken using the constitutional powers then in the province's hands.

1. Withdraw from the Canada Pension Plan to create an Alberta plan offering the same benefits at lower cost, while giving Alberta some control over the investment fund.

2. Collect our own revenue from personal income tax, as Alberta already does for corporate income tax, basing the potential policy flexibility on Quebec's experience.

3. Create an Alberta Provincial Police Force in 2012, when the RCMP contract with the province runs out.

4. Resume provincial responsibility for health care policy — fighting it in court if Ottawa objects.

5. Use Section 88 of the Supreme Court's decision in the Quebec Secession Reference to force Senate reform back onto the national agenda.

The "firewall" letter was frequently used in subsequent leadership races and, occasionally in the 2004 election, by both eastern Conservatives and Liberals to peg Harper as too western, too provincial rights oriented, to be a national leader. His defence has generally been to note that, in the letter and in other policy statements, he has limited his aspirations for Alberta to those already claimed by Quebec under currently held constitutional powers available to all provinces.

On December 14, 2004, Harper made a major address on foreign policy issues to the Canadian Club in Ottawa. It was a year since the Alliance and Conservative Parties had merged, nine months since he himself had won the new party's leadership, six months since the 2004 election in which the Conservatives had won ninety-nine seats, and three months before their inaugural policy conference in Montreal.

Harper used the occasion to quote Preston Manning a bit, and Brian Mulroney extensively, to bring a historical imprint to the party's foreign affairs stance, "For Conserva-tives, the defining element of our approach to foreign policy is to better advance the national interest, including the security of Canadian territory; the economic prosperity of the Canadian people; and the values of democracy, freedom and compassion that define the Canadian nation." The nod to former leaders of the party's merged elements came as Harper talked about the need for a comprehensive security partnership with the United States. "As Preston Manning once said, in a different context, we have to 'think big' on this, our most important relationship." That paved the way for the reference to the former Conservative prime minister: "As Brian Mulroney showed, to make progress with the Americans, we have to be confident, open, and aggressive. [His] most lasting achievement was continental free trade, based on exploiting North American opportunity and reality. Even with the Liberals standing absolutely still, Canada-U.S. trade has doubled in dollar volume since 1994, with some $2 billion in trade crossing the border each day." He suggested that he had "inherited" a proud conservative tradition of "constructive internationalism": "The Mulroney Conservative government record in development assistance and international security was a record of success. Beginning with John Diefenbaker, Canada led the fight against apartheid in South Africa. Mr. Mulroney vigorously widened this policy, disagreeing with the United States without being disagreeable, without in any way jeopardizing our bilateral relationship."

The significance of the Mulroney reference was tied to two points. The first was the need to provide some *gravitas* and historical context to party policy on foreign affairs, since a "government-in-waiting" gets asked some of its most serious questions in that field. The second was that Harper, working toward his first policy conference, needed to "look forward by looking back." True, he was the first leader of the newly merged party, but he was also inheriting a tradition that in one case (Reform) went back fifteen years and in the other (Conservative) dated back to Confederation.

Furthermore, Mulroney was emerging from the unfounded accusations that had been levelled by the Liberals early in Jean Chrétien's tenure with respect to what had been called the "Airbus" affair. Having won a multimillion dollar settlement from the government, in connection with its making public a seemingly incriminating letter from the RCMP about an Airbus investigation, he was coming back into respect in the party that he had led for a decade.

Some readers may have noticed an emphasis in this book

on the Preston Manning–Reform legacy with which Harper has worked. That emphasis, which grows out of my observation of federal politics over the past fifteen years, should not diminish the fact that the current progress of the Conservative Party relates to bringing together both the Mulroney and the Manning legacies.

When it came to the same-sex marriage issue, Harper managed to encourage a "middle of the road" position that provided clear opposition to the Liberal plan to redefine marriage, but he also provided a clear option for the courts to look at should "equality" become an issue in the future. Writing in the *Ottawa Citizen* on February 18, 2005, Harper noted that

> It will come as no surprise to anybody to know that I support the traditional definition of marriage as a union of one man and one woman to the exclusion of all others, as expressed in our traditional common law. I believe this definition of marriage has served society well, has stood the test of time, and is, in fact, a foundational institution of society.
>
> In my view, the onus is on those who want to overturn such a fundamental social institution to prove that it is absolutely necessary, that there is no other compromise that can respect the rights of same-sex couples while still preserving one of the cornerstones of our society and its many cultures.

Harper reflected here the views of about one-third of Canadians as expressed in polls and surveys: they supported the traditional definition of marriage but had no objection to equality for nontraditional unions. That position was not acceptable to strongly doctrinaire socons, particularly those who adhered to the Vatican stance, which maintained that no Catholic politician should support legislation that legitimized other kinds of unions.

Be that as it may, Harper maintained, with respect to same-sex unions,

> We would propose that other forms of union, however structured, by appropriate provincial legislation, whether called registered partnerships, domestic partnerships, civil union or whatever, should be entitled to the same legal rights, privileges, and obligations as marriage.
>
> Many of these types of unions are already subject to provincial jurisdiction under their responsibility for civil law. However, there are issues affecting rights and benefits within the federal domain, and our party would ensure that for all federal purposes those Canadians living in other forms of union would be recognized as having equal rights and benefits under federal law as well.

Harper also made the point that no national or international court or human rights tribunal, at the national or international level, "has ever ruled that same-sex marriage is a human right."

Harper's "pilgrimage" from a grounding in a relatively narrow conservative focus to a broader cultural context was a key element in helping to shake loose the "hidden agenda" branding.

Simon Fraser University economist Herb Grubel, a Reform MP at the same time as Harper, suggests that he trusts Harper because he knows him, at the base, to be both a knowledgeable economist and a libertarian. Whatever else he may be, Grubel suggests, the Conservative leader will be good for Canada as a prime minister because of his professional competence and his sense that less government is better government.

So Harper proved himself adept at nuancing his views as different groups of people showed up at the conservative table and a variety of issues called for means by which conservatives could enhance, rather than demonize, the various participants in their partnership. In the next chapter, I will chronicle the several stages of the Conservative merger.

CHAPTER NINE

Elders and Angels

On June 18, 2003, I attended a barbecue for press gallery members at Stornoway, the official residence of the opposition leader. This annual event, like a similar occasion at 24 Sussex Drive, the prime minister's residence, is a chance for reporters to compare notes and see what the hosting politicians seemed to be hinting at.

Harper and Jim Armour, at the time his communications director, happened by, and we exchanged pleasantries. Then I offered a comment and asked a question. The comment, in short form, went like this: "Last Saturday night, at the press gallery dinner, you did a great impersonation of Preston Manning, in which you quoted him as saying 'We need to be uniiiiters, rather than diviiiiders.' Then, two nights later, speaking to one thousand business leaders in Toronto, you repeated the unity sentiments, without the Manning mimic."

To see my comment in context, we need to recall that, when Stephen Harper ran for the Canadian Alliance leadership, just a little over a year before, joining the Alliance with the Progressive Conservatives was not the top plank on his platform. Furthermore, it seemed that CA members did not see unity as a top priority. In fact, the two unity candidates, Diane Ablonczy and Grant Hill, drew less than ten percent of the vote combined in the contest, while Harper took close to fifty-five percent of the vote.

My question was "What is going on? One night you utter statements that are funny and not necessarily true. Two nights later your statements are intended to be true but not necessarily funny." Harper and Armour both smiled and took on the satisfied appearance of cats who had swallowed mice.

By fall, word was out that senior prominent Alliance and Conservative "emissaries" had been working all summer, under cover of the seasonal doldrums, to come up with a plan for a merger of the Canadian Alliance and federal Progressive Conservative Parties. By December, it was a done deal, and three months later Harper became leader of the new party. He appointed Peter MacKay as deputy leader.

The "impossible" had happened. Harper had confounded his critics and even mildly surprised his supporters. He was beginning to show the attributes that many of those supporters had spoken of when they had touted him as a future leader. He seemed strongly anchored to his conservative principles and strategically pragmatic in applying those beliefs. He was ready now to see whether strong doses of incrementalism could bring a conservative government back to power in Canada.

Harper operated within a dichotomy in pulling together the new Conservative Party. On the one hand, he and MacKay clandestinely gathered several elderly white gentlemen — seasoned political advisors — in the summer of 2003 to advise them on the proposed merger. On the other hand, and almost as quietly, Harper, with MacKay's aid and approval, brought together a caucus that, compared with the doddering governing Liberals, was bright, energetic, feisty, young, and conservative.

Among the latter group was a strong contingent of women. Some, such as Ablonczy, had been part of the "Class of '93." She had earned her spurs not only as a formidable debater and questioner in the House but also, prior to election, as the first president and later communications director of the Reform Party. Others, such as Carol Skelton (whose riding is Saskatoon-Rosetown-Biggar) and Lynne Yelich (representing Blackstrap, also a Saskatoon riding), had been in place from 1997 on. Harper had, in effect, inherited Ablonczy, Yelich, and Skelton from Manning.

But it was one of the new recruits, Rona (pronounced "rawna,") Ambrose, who signalled the coalescing of what *Ottawa Citizen* reporter Norma Greenaway described as "Harper's Angels." Ambrose, thirty-five, was a constitutional advisor to Alberta Premier Ralph Klein before being elected as a Conservative MP from Edmonton–Spruce Grove in 2004. And she found her way onto the radar screen on February 15, 2005, when she rose in Question Period to tell hockey legend Ken Dryden, fifty-seven, that Canadian working mothers did not need "old white guys" to tell them how to organize their child care. Dryden, as social development minister, was negotiating his national child care plans with the provinces at the time. Her comment received critical acclaim for chutzpah on at least two significant grounds.

The first was that Ambrose used statistics from a Vanier Institute of the Family survey to argue that most young couples would like to have at least one parent stay at home with the children during their first few years, or at least make their own child care arrangements outside the home, rather than put their children in state-run institutions. She likely knew that a Vanier survey was a good arrow to use in piercing Dryden's armour, because he himself was on the institute's board of directors.

The second was that her argument was patently conservative — arguing for the traditional family. It struck a blow against the sometimes conventional wisdom that to be "with it" one had to be a Liberal and antitraditional. Particularly galling to many conservatives is the kind of state-run daycare system that would replace parental influence with state indoctrination as a tool for child development. That idea conjures up the Cold War–era, anticommunist imagery of Marxist-dominated state nurseries that allegedly prevailed in the Soviet Union, maintained so that mothers would be "free" to sweep Moscow sidewalks or clean the public latrines — all under threat of exile to Siberia and permanent separation from their progeny.

While Ambrose's remarks stopped well short of communicating that imagery, they triggered some journalistic punditry that led to the "discovery" of these heretofore ignored smart, striking, and unabashedly conservative women. And less than a month later, on March 12, Greenaway's article appeared in the *Ottawa Citizen*. It was repeated three days later in the *National Post*. The headline was a takeoff on the *Charlie's Angels* television show of twenty-five years ago, which featured three bright young women who solved crimes at the behest of a mysterious older boss identified only by his telephone voice. The old white guys would remember the show; Harper and most of his angels were likely at various stages of teenhood at the time. The *Citizen/Post* story featured a photo by Wayne Cuddington that showed most of the women in question clustered around a smiling and only slightly sheepish Harper under one of the Parliament buildings' gothic-arched casement windows. Absent from the shoot were Rona Ambrose and Belinda Stronach, whose headshots were included in the body of the story, and Bev Oda, who received story mention.

The angels included

- Diane Ablonczy (Calgary–Nose Hill, Alberta)
- Rona Ambrose (Edmonton–Spruce Grove, Alberta)
- Diane Finley (Haldimand-Norfolk, Ontario)
- Cheryl Gallant (Renfrew-Nipissing-Pembroke, Ontario)
- Helena Guergis (Simcoe-Grey, Ontario)
- Nina Grewal (Fleetwood–Port Kells, British Columbia)
- Betty Hinton (Kamloops-Thompson-Cariboo, British Columbia)
- Bev Oda (Durham, Ontario)
- Carol Skelton (Saskatoon-Rosetown-Biggar, Saskatchewan)
- Joy Smith (Kildonan–St. Paul, Manitoba)

- Belinda Stronach (Newmarket-Aurora, Ontario)
- Josee Verner (appointed Quebec caucus representative)
- Lynne Yelich (Blackstrap, Saskatchewan)

(A few months later, of course, Stronach was receiving new titles other than angel.)

A study of the people on the Greenaway list reveals particular roles for the angels. Ablonczy, Hinton, Skelton, and Yelich were the experienced members. Ambrose and Guergis are the social moderates, the chic, sharp women whose pre-Commons experience gave them the confidence to speak strongly from the get-go. Oda, as a former CRTC commissioner, as well as a member with Japanese parentage, gave the party someone who could respond strongly to critics who saw Conservatives as automatically anti-arts and anti-ethnic. Verner had a unique role in that she was not elected but had the particular task of liaising with Quebec, represented only by Liberals and the Bloc. Newcomers Finley and Smith were seen as solid constituency people. And Grewal was being watched as the female half of the first married couple to sit in the House at the same time.

In this treatise, I am using the terms "elders" and "angels" to provide continuity with the stridently collaborative imagery sometimes associated with religious practice. The emissaries, or elders as I am calling them, were all "old white guys." There were two modest exceptions: Ottawa-area MP Scott Reid, a youngish white guy who had constitutional and business backgrounds to belie his age, and Senator Gerry St. Germain, who has considerable Métis heritage. As senior statespersons in various sectors of the conservative movement, elders had congenial clout. And they needed it. Furthermore, they had the tacit blessing of either Preston Manning or Brian Mulroney, who at that point were singing from the same hymnbook on merger issues, albeit in different pews.

But the elders also had to help Harper and MacKay climb out of a hole that MacKay had dug when he had won the leadership of the Progressive Conservative Party in May 2003. That was when, to ensure his election over Calgary's Jim Prentice, he struck a deal with David Orchard, the third runner and far-left Tory who had run on an anti-free-trade, no-truck-or-trade-with-the-Alliance platform. In the hastily scribbled-and-signed deal, MacKay vowed not to negotiate with the Alliance, although he crossed out a reference to refusing to hold talks with that party.

MacKay's move was widely described as a "deal with the devil." Although it was seen as having played a role in his election as leader, it also gave MacKay the clear appearance of someone who chose expediency over the good of the party. Many in his party told him quietly that he had no business signing such an agreement. But what was to be done?

The answer, in effect, was to choose some wise and seasoned conservatives who had no baggage on either side of the Conservative-Alliance issue to talk tough, bang a few heads together, listen and console, and do whatever else was needed to make this thing happen. MacKay needed these "keepers of the flame" to quietly admit that his deal with Orchard, whatever its value in the short term, could not be countenanced by his elders. The six emissaries (with some of their formal and informal credentials mentioned) were as follows.

• *Tory MP Loyola Hearn.* From Newfoundland, Hearn was the Newfoundland and Labrador education minister before entering federal politics. He was seen as being knowledgeable about the Atlantic Canadian culture that was part of MacKay's background. In particular, he could advise Harper, who had leapt into some hot water in Atlantic Canada for suggesting that Liberal-inspired welfare policies had created a "culture of failure" in the region.

• *Former Ontario Premier Bill Davis.* Now close to eighty, Davis is the longest in the tooth of the elders. He was considered one of the most successful Ontario politicians and one who readily understood what it would take to get conservatives in his province to quit parking their federal votes with the Liberals. A moderately devout United Church member, he has a fair understanding of what it takes to make a more liberal form of religion work alongside a conservative political process.

• *Former federal cabinet minister Don Mazankowski.* The closest of the group to Brian Mulroney, Mazankowski, from Edmonton, held the finance and deputy prime minister portfolios in his cabinet. He was in the House of Commons when Deborah Grey was the lone Reformer and well understood the Reform-Tory tensions from the Conservative side. He grew up on an Alberta farm, the son of Polish immigrants.

• *Ray Speaker, a former Reform Party MP.* Speaker could be seen as the person best able to interpret Manning to the group. He had the distinction of having served in the Alberta provincial cabinets of Ernest Manning (Preston's father) and Conservative Don Getty. Furthermore, he was an evangelical Christian who understood that religious culture.

• *Current Ottawa-area Alliance MP Scott Reid.* Reid is a scion of the family that runs the Giant Tiger discount store chain. And he has written extensively on Canadian constitutional matters. Less known is the fact that he is Jewish and played a role in helping to build relations between conservatives in the Jewish community and the Canadian Alliance.

• *Senator Gerry St. Germain.* A Mulroney cabinet minister and Senate appointee, St. Germain is a devoutly conservative Roman Catholic and has Métis ancestry. At the time of the formation of the Canadian Alliance, he decided to sit as an Alliance member in the Senate, thus enabling him to be part of the CA caucus. All the while, his office sported a three-foot-high portrait of Mulroney in its entranceway.

So, both culturally and politically, the elders enjoyed gap-bridging prowess to advise Harper and MacKay. And the angels, as well as their young male counterparts, helped to brand the new party as, well, "new," as well as fresh, articulate, and ready for the future.

For Harper, as leader, the presence of the "elders" meant that he had grasped the need to be mentored not just by the Calgary School but also by people of experience in both the Conservative and the Alliance Parties. It marked his progress toward building a large and far-ranging "sounding board."

And, in turn, he was moving into a role that made it possible for him to mentor the younger people who could, in due course, be in a Conservative cabinet both in the near future and many years from now.

CHAPTER TEN

The Belinda Factor

Stephen Harper has become renowned for a bland and cool demeanour. There has been a regular litany of complaints from journalists about their difficulty in finding warm and fuzzy stories about Harper; they say that his shows of emotion have been too few and far between. Indeed, some of the grim-faced anger that Harper showed during the charges of Liberal corruption emerging from the Gomery Commission was seen as a major reason why the public could not "connect" with him. Not to show suitable anger, perhaps even growly grumbling, was to trivialize Liberal malfeasance. But there have been a fair number of instances of determination, both congenial and grim, showing that Harper indeed has both personality and emotions.

On October 16, 2003, Peter MacKay and Stephen Harper jointly announced an agreement to seek a merger of the Canadian Alliance and Progressive Conservative Parties. It had been a whirlwind process, with packs of journalists chasing the two leaders back and forth across the country, trying to find out the latest information. As the previous chapter noted, the process had been taken forward through the on again, off again, involvement of the "emissaries," the six senior statespersons from "politics past" who had hammered out a framework to let Harper and MacKay talk.

Harper, particularly, astounded the pundits with his persistence, given that he had less to lose if the merger did not happen. With boyish enthusiasm, he caught a plane headed for Atlantic Canada one evening, chasing an elusive MacKay so he could pin him down. And it was that boyishness that emerged on the morning of October 16. "I could hardly sleep last night," he intoned in a manner that belied youthful excitement. "It is like Christmas morning!" MacKay, the younger of the two men, was much more the "cool cat."

Much has been made of Harper's bland appearance even under great pressure. He makes fun of it himself when staring at an audience and, without moving any more facial muscles than it takes to get words out of his mouth, declares in quick order, "This is Stephen Harper ecstatic. This is Stephen Harper angry. This is Stephen Harper perplexed." But there are times when he lights up. And, at other times, he portrays a grim-faced determination. Not when he is in control of the situation, but when he needs it to complete what he is doing.

That happened one night during the 2004 election campaign when he accepted, without the full backing of his handlers, the task of pitching the first ball at a Toronto Blue Jays baseball game in the SkyDome. The backroom guys cautioned that it had been Robert Stanfield's dropping of a football, three decades before, that had marked him, unfairly or otherwise, as a fumbler who could not match the agile Pierre Elliott Trudeau. Harper pressed ahead, however. And, as it happened, he got the baseball across the plate.

And the image captured for the newspapers the next day was one of grim determination. It was as if he believed he could will the ball to go where he wanted it to. Readers will know the expression "It is all in how you hold your tongue" when trying to perform a delicate mechanical task in a tight spot. Harper's equivalent to tongue holding is teeth-gritting, lip-pursing, mind-focusing face fortification.

And later there was the chair-kicking incident at the 2005 Conservative policy convention in Montreal. There is nothing on film to prove it, but CPAC journalists swear it happened. Momentarily angry over some of the convention agenda items not quite falling into place, the opposition leader took out his exasperation on the nearest inanimate object. The incident shows that Harper is not the emotionless persona he tries to cultivate. On some occasions, he has a quick temper — quick to rise and just as quick to simmer down.

On other occasions, he is boyishly delighted. His face lights up when a colleague has performed well or done something to please him. The person on the receiving end of the smile knows without question that Harper is pleased.

But always he moves back quickly to the task at hand. No time to waste in reaching the next objective. What is required is clear thinking, good research, and, once more, determination to reach the goal.

All of this consideration brings us to the June 28, 2004, election and Harper's disappointment, his disappearance, and the rumours of his resignation. The election seemed to send Harper into a period of deep introspection. His demeanour, the few times he appeared in public right after the election, betrayed disappointment, perhaps even a bit of depression. Harper spoke of taking some time off to determine if he would remain leader, and the expression on his face when he said so seemed to say, "Don't be surprised if I don't stay."

Was Harper about to head back to Calgary, once again disgusted and disappointed with federal politics as he saw it? Was he blaming himself for the loss, wondering if he had miscalculated in not taking a sea-to-sea tour or concentrating on some key Ontario ridings in those last days before June 28?

The Ontario situation was especially troubling. Ten days before the vote, the polls were showing a possible fifty seats in the most populous province. The final result was half that. It was like the glass that is both half full and half empty. The Conservatives had reason to be happy about an Ontario breakthrough. It demonstrated, in one respect at least, that the merger had been a good idea, because the Alliance/Tory vote splitting had finally come to a screeching halt. Most analysis of the 2000 election had shown that at least twenty of the Liberal seats were the result of such splitting — especially in the capital area and parts of southwestern Ontario. True, a further twenty-five seats in Ontario would have given the Conservatives a small edge — a chance to govern as a minority, with all its risks and rewards.

But now Harper faced reality, not what could have been.

He had not won a minority government, and he was deeply disappointed. But once he emerged from his hiatus, he drew strength from having a shadow cabinet whose members were young, experienced, energetic, and acting like they wanted real cabinet posts.

Which brings us to the next major blindside — the defection of Belinda Stronach to the Liberals.

Once Harper had made it plain that he was remaining in the leadership and pulled together his shadow cabinet, six weeks after the 2004 election, Plan A seemed to be falling into place. Jim Armour, who had been his communications director, was moved laterally into a new official opposition department called public affairs. No longer would Armour have direct contact with the media on a daily basis. Now his task was to rebrand the Conservative caucus as the "government-in-waiting." He was replaced by Geoff Norquay, a veteran and savvy communications person from the Progressive Conservative side of the now disassembled fence.

Announcement of the shadow cabinet was designed to reinforce the government-in-waiting image and the implicit assumption that, in minority government situations, the "wait" might be short or long. The event itself could not take place at Rideau Hall because there was no cause for the governor general to swear in those who would be cross-checking the cabinet ministers in Parliament. The cabinet swearing in always included a photo opportunity with the new and reminted ministers lined up on risers and the prime minister planted smiling in the centre of the front row. Harper, Armour, and Norquay picked the ornate and magisterial Room 200, in the West Block of the parliamentary complex, to announce the shadow cabinet. And the risers were in place there as they had been a few weeks before at Rideau Hall for the Liberal swearing in.

Noted by several journalists was the fact that few old Reform or Alliance MPs were on the opposition front benches, so to speak. The clear message seemed to be that, if the cultures of the two founding parties — and the five or six different kinds of conservatism — were going to come together, the socons needed to step back a bit and let the party's centre and more left elements share the spotlight.

Belinda Stronach was on the front bench with the international business shadow portfolio. She was positioned to draw from her private sector experience in her father's corporate world.

Furthermore, as noted earlier, Stronach was made the benchmate, in the House of Commons, of Stockwell Day, the best-known social conservative, who had been rehabilitating himself, after his disastrous run as Alliance leader, in the foreign affairs shadow portfolio. He was, in fact, acquitting himself quite well. His bridge-building with the conservative Jewish community has been well-publicized. What is less known is that he has worked quietly to understand the Muslim perspective, as well.

Most of the common intelligence seemed to point to letting the government stand for at least eighteen months to two years. But all that began to change once the Gomery Commission ploughed on with its work, beginning in the fall of 2004. The Conservative shift toward trying to bring down the government sooner intensified in the spring of 2005 with the daily evidence, both documentation and testimony, of a scandal involving at least $300 million in payments to Liberal-friendly advertising agencies. Those payments were apparently in the interest of promoting Canadian unity in the wake of the close call in the 1995 Quebec Sovereignty Referendum. Further fuelling the scandal was extensive testimony that some of those payments — for little or no real work — were being kicked back to Liberal Party coffers, many of them in secret or under-the-table "passalongs."

Harper, buoyed by periodic indications that Liberal popularity was declining, began to drop hints about a possible defeat of the government on the floor of the House. But when Minister of Finance Ralph Goodale brought forward the budget on February 23, 2005, Harper indicated that he actually liked many of its features, including proposed tax rate cuts. A few days later, on the budget's first reading, the Tories remained in their seats rather than either support or oppose it.

Some of the Tory leader's reticence may have related to the fact that the Conservative policy convention was still ahead, and perhaps Harper wanted to get a little firmer reading on just how much his caucus — and the party as a whole — would support whatever he might do. After the convention, with an eighty-four percent backing from delegates, and a platform that included items to please most sectors of conservatism, Harper returned to Ottawa in a slightly feistier mood.

Furthermore, his previous lukewarm acceptance of the Liberal budget turned to clear opposition when the prime minister struck a deal with NDP leader Jack Layton to boost spending by $4.6 billion and strike down proposed tax rate cuts for corporations. Harper now believed he had strong grounds on which to oppose the budget. Not only had the

Liberals lost the moral authority to govern, on the basis of having called the last election before the Gomery Commission could do its work, but now the government was adopting a tax-and-spend regime to win support from the political left.

While the "blame" for wanting to trigger an early election seemed, on the surface, to lie with Harper himself, there was some evidence that much of the enthusiasm came from the socon flank, who were still not quite comfortable with their colleagues on the left of the party. The thinking seemed to be that an early election would either confirm Harper as the longer-term leader or, given a Conservative defeat, open the way for electing a "real" socon leader.

Be that as it may, the Tory caucus unanimously backed their leader on the strategy of trying to bring down the government and trigger a spring election. But Stronach publicly expressed misgivings about the strategy, claiming that many people in her Toronto suburban riding needed the kinds of fiscal goodies the Liberals were promising.

Of course, from the very beginning, many Conservatives, both socon and fiscon, were suspicious that Stronach was an unreconstructed Liberal — a Trojan Horse in the Tory camp, so to speak. Moreover, her romantic relationship with deputy leader Peter MacKay, and her penchant for dazzling parties, were seen by a fair number of fellow party members as attempts to undermine Harper's ability to bring the various facets of the party together. And then, on the morning of May 17, 2005, the prime minister and Stronach strode into a hastily called press conference and jointly announced that she was crossing the floor and would become the new Liberal human resources and skills development minister.

For several days, the expressed Tory acrimony for Stronach ran hot and heavy.

Along with that came Peter MacKay's obvious distress at the ending of their romance. Close to the surface, in that part of the saga, was the emotional support that Stephen and Laureen provided for MacKay in the immediate follow-up to the floor-crossing breakup. It was a natural development. While the rapport between MacKay and Harper was not always perfectly harmonious, the two men had, in the merger process, become good friends. The trust was building, and Harper depended on MacKay, on a fairly regular basis, to speak for the Conservatives in places where the deputy leader's words would carry the day. Harper did other little things to let MacKay know that he trusted him. There were times, for example, when Harper moved MacKay further up on the Question Period agenda — from, say, seventh spot to second — than those handling the agenda had originally proposed.

And, shortly after the Montreal convention, where MacKay created a bit of a dustup on a delegation-assignment proposal, Harper quickly squelched rumours that he was seeing his deputy's issues as threatening to his own position. Harper did so with an extension of personal trust. Harper made a public point that MacKay would be his "hockey dad" stand-in at the press-politician game where his son Benjamin was playing centre for the politicians.

Earlier in the process of this trust building, however, one question had lurked. Would MacKay contest the leadership against Harper? Or, if not, would he support another candidate — maybe Stronach? On January 13, 2004, MacKay settled the matter. In a press conference attended by his then five-year partner, Lisa Merrithew, he noted that he was not running. And he pointed out that he had made the decision in church that weekend after considerable soul-searching. He noted cryptically that he had discovered, in the process, that he had a soul — which many Conservatives had suggested he had "sold" in turning on his agreement with David Orchard not to have truck or trade with the Canadian Alliance.

Significant about that press conference was the obvious chemistry — at that time — between MacKay and Merrithew: her eye contact with him and her obvious happiness with the decision he had made, and his own clearly stated love and appreciation for his partner and her steadfast support. A few months later they were no longer an item. In January 2005, during the Conservative caucus meeting in Victoria, Peter and Belinda went public with their relationship.

All of this is significant in the Harper story because, at the right moments, Stephen and Laureen have modelled the traditional family to MacKay. What he does with it, ultimately, given that he has reached two decades of adulthood without the joys and encumbrances of marriage, is perhaps a moot question.

It seems that the kind of tradition and stability that Harper, along with his wife's behind-the-scenes support, has brought to the Conservative caucus did not fit particularly well with Stronach's plans or, for that matter, did not gel with her skills and mindset. That possibility brings us to a column written by veteran former MP and journalist Doug Fisher a few days after Stronach jumped ship. In a May 21 piece written for the Canoe.com network (Sun Media), he dismissed some of the anti-female sentiments that had been tossed around in previous days, insisting instead that

Stronach was, in effect, miscast as a "political animal." Noted Fisher, "Over the 16 months since she walked onto the public stage, Belinda Stronach has shown no improvement as a prospect for great work in the highest places." After talking about all the things she had going for her — wealth, powerful family, friends in high places — he suggested that

> She is not cut out for the game of politics. She's just not a "natural" — unlike women such as the late Judy La Marsh, or Deborah Grey and Sheila Copps. More than a year of generous exposure by the news media demonstrates that she is barely an adequate speaker, let alone a good one.
>
> She cannot think on her feet and has a relentless devotion to clichés and chamber of commerce platitudes.
>
> This does not mean she's stupid or slow or short on energy. But she is unready — and probably never will be — for able, heavy, cabinet-level responsibility and leadership.

Stronach's strengths and weaknesses together provide some clues to what her potential usefulness in the public sphere might be. Stronach played a key role in bringing together the Alliance and the Conservatives. But she was clearly uncomfortable in articulating conservative philosophy and even more so in attacking liberal or left-leaning action. That reluctance spelled trouble for her working within an opposition setting — thus the reason for her striking out at Harper.

In terms of political philosophy, Stronach has emerged in a way that several words could, at least with partial accuracy, describe: impartial, nonaligned, on the fence, indistinct, indeterminate. No wonder that she could not hit it off with the person the Conservatives chose to be their leader. Harper needs to be the opposition leader and the "prime minister" of the government-in-waiting. Yes, he has an important role to play in a minority Parliament in getting conservative-minded amendments into Liberal legislation. Harper cannot afford to play the role the NDP has adopted and, if anything, needs to work at getting conservative antidotes into a tax-and-spend budget organized in part by Jack Layton and his labour leader sidekick, Buzz Hargrove.

Much has been said, with some validity, about modelling the current minority Parliament on that of the Lester Pearson years in the late 1960s. There are some significant differences, however, in the dynamics that prevailed then and those occurring today.

Pearson's modus operandi, as a career diplomat, was to work with both the NDP on the left and the Social Credit on the right to bring forward legislation that would, to some degree, satisfy both. That left the Diefenbaker Conservatives to function as the official opposition, while the Liberals, in effect, governed with the tacit permission of smaller parties at each end of the political spectrum.

An intriguing story coming out of the Pearson years points up the particular minority dynamics that prevailed at that time. It focuses on the adoption of the Maple Leaf and the retirement of its predecessor, the Red Ensign, as the Canadian flag. The story became available to me as a result of certain entries in the Robert Thompson archives at Trinity

Western University. When the new flag was hoisted atop the Parliament buildings in Ottawa on February 15, 1965, Pearson, as a token of friendship, gave Thompson the Red Ensign that had flown over the West Block. That ensign now rests in the Trinity Western archives, accompanied by the story of how the Pearson Parliament adopted the new flag. Karla Keeping, a Trinity Western communications officer, pulled together the story from the Thompson archives as a "special interest" piece for the TWU website for Canada Day 2005, marking the forty years since the Maple Leaf first flew.

> Pearson was determined that Canada have a distinctive national flag, but the opposition continually delayed the debate most likely in an ongoing effort to dissolve the minority government.
>
> In 1964 a flag committee consisting of representatives from all parties was established and given six weeks to resolve the flag issue. The group held 45 meetings, heard 12 expert witnesses and received approximately 2000 submissions from across the country. Ninety of those designs were up for debate, three of which Thompson himself submitted.
>
> The Conservatives knew Pearson strongly favoured the flag design with three maple leaves, and as a result, the Conservatives strongly opposed it. But what they didn't know was that the single maple leaf design — a design Pearson wasn't too fond of — had been submitted anonymously by Liberal and committee member John Matheson in an attempt to bridge Pearson's choice of flag with other opinions in the group. Matheson knew that if the committee

could not agree, Canada would not have a new flag, and the indecision would reflect poorly on the competence of the minority government.

It came down to three flag prototypes: (1) those with three maple leaves; (2) those with a single maple leaf; and (3) those with the Union Jack, the Fleur-de-lis or a combination of the two. Information taken from Pearson's private memoirs shows that though Pearson personally preferred the flag with three maple leaves, he secretly agreed to compromise and support the single maple leaf flag. When it came time to vote for the flag, expecting to oppose the Liberals, the Conservatives on the committee all voted for the single maple leaf. The shocked and startled Conservatives watched as the Liberals and the minor opposition parties also voted in favour of the same flag, as they had already agreed among themselves to do. So the Maple Leaf flag went forward on a unanimous vote, giving us the Maple Leaf flag we have today.

The Maple Leaf was selected in "the most democratic way anything ever passed in Parliament," said Thompson in an interview in 1995, though he recalls that Conservative leader John Diefenbaker was so upset about the outcome that he refused to attend the ceremony February 15. For Thompson, the Red Ensign symbolized an important part of history, and that's probably why he wanted to keep the flag.

The story in effect illustrates both the personal and the political dynamics that made the Pearson Parliament different from what currently prevails. On the personal level,

Pearson, the diplomat who respected Thompson's previous leadership in the Ethiopian educational system after World War II, had little trouble winning his support as well as that of Tommy Douglas in the NDP. On the political level, that made John Diefenbaker the "odd man out."

But keep in mind as well that Diefenbaker, unlike Harper, had already had his stint as prime minister, from 1958 to 1963. He was at that stage in life where he was the curmudgeonly "Dief the Chief," and the knives were out within the Conservative Party to replace him. For Harper, his government is still in waiting, and the Tory knives will not be unsheathed until he has either served a few years as prime minister or failed in the quest.

In the Martin minority, there is no smaller conservative party to hold the balance of power. Instead, there is a separatist party, the Bloc Québécois, which owes its current strength to being the Quebec force against Liberal corruption. There is no incentive for the Bloc to vote with the government, so Parliament ends up as an almost even balance between a centre-left de facto coalition and an opposition itself split between conservatives on the one hand and separatists on the other.

Harper works with the challenge of leading a broadly based party in an adversarial House. He needs to exercise the discipline that will keep the party together, yet he cannot relent on opposing the government or, at the most, damning it occasionally with faint praise.

But does that mean Stronach is good for nothing in the world of politics? Perhaps not. She could have an impartial, indistinct, nonaligned, albeit significant, role to play once she is able to wind away from whatever created her conflict with the party she helped to found. Indeed, her salvation could be in the second role that Paul Martin gave her — that of "democratic renewal."

* * *

This thought occurred to me because of time spent in the early part of 2005 in British Columbia teaching political journalism at Trinity Western University. Each year, the university hosts the Mel Smith Memorial Lecture. The 2005 lecture was given by Kenneth Carty, former chair of the University of British Columbia political science department and, more significantly for our present purposes, chief research officer for the Citizens' Assembly on Electoral Reform. The assembly had been activated by B.C. Premier Gordon Campbell and was chosen randomly to bring forward recommendations for making electoral democracy work more effectively at the provincial level.

Campbell wanted to eliminate the wrinkles in the electoral system that led to anomalies such as "wrong party" and "landslide" elections, each of which produced results in spades within the past decade in British Columbia. The "wrong party" election in 1996 produced an NDP government with thirty-seven percent of the popular vote, four percent less than the Liberals received. In 1991, with just fifty-seven percent of the popular vote, the Liberals turned the tables, winning seventy-seven of seventy-nine seats.

At the Mel Smith lecture, Carty talked about the recommendations that the Citizens' Assembly produced, wrapped in a package known as the "Single Transferable Vote" or STV. In brief, the STV concept calls for the reduction in the number of ridings from seventy-nine to fifteen, with several legislators elected from each enlarged riding. Voters would mark the candidates' names in order of preference, and the vote count would be based on applying the preferences to complete the election process.

Carty maintained that the STV system would tend to reduce and indeed come close to eliminating the chances of wrong party or landslide results. It would make coalitions more likely, allow small parties to have some representation in the legislature, and lead to "collaborative" politics, rather than adversarialism, as the order of the day.

Carty allowed that it took a randomly chosen citizens' group, rather than a parliamentary committee, to express a desire for collaboration. Indeed, he noted that parliamentary committees looking into electoral reform in Quebec, New Brunswick, and Prince Edward Island have been much less innovative and consequently less successful in reaching some new thinking on electoral reform.

The STV was a ballot item in the May 17, 2005, B.C. election. While the vote in favour of the concept was not enough to meet the threshold that had been required to make its implementation mandatory, it was strong enough that West Coast politicians will know better than to let it die a natural death.

* * *

Perhaps Stronach could invest some time and money looking into what happened in British Columbia to see if such electoral reform could happen at the federal level. And Harper might keep in mind that Stronach's usefulness to the body politic might not yet be over.

While the discussion of Stronach is a bit of a diversion from the recounting of Harper's pilgrimage, it provides a useful lead into the final chapter, which will try to envision how a Harper prime ministership might play out.

CHAPTER ELEVEN

From Here on In

I write this final chapter in the midst of a flurry over whether devout Christian people backed by organizations that have a clear pro-life and pro-family agenda should be permitted to run candidates for the Conservative Party. The final outcome of this issue, as it relates to the ability of Stephen Harper to lead the Conservatives into government at the next election, highlights once again that this story is, in part at least, about the interfacing of faith and politics at the federal level. Thus, the concept of Harper's story as a pilgrimage is borne out.

Before dealing directly and finally with the question of how the six different kinds of conservatives function within the new Conservative Party, I would like to tell the story of

Walter Block. He personifies the interface of faith and politics in the fiscally conservative sector. A piece entitled "Walter Block and the Budget Vote" that I wrote on May 18, 2005, for my weekly Ottawa*Watch* analysis for religious leaders tells his story.

> An examination of Stephen Harper's grounding in fiscal conservatism — as well as a little story about Walter Block — goes some distance to explain why the Conservative leader has made it such a point to try bringing down the minority Liberals on the corruption/budget issue cluster.
>
> In 1991, Harper completed his master's degree in economics from the University of Calgary by defending his thesis.
>
> The main burden of that thesis was to examine the assumption that governments upset the natural time cycle of our market economy by inordinate spending in pre-election periods.
>
> Harper's thinking, in that thesis and in his subsequent activity as an economist, in both the political and the advocacy spheres, is rooted in the kind of fiscal conservatism in which he has steeped himself.
>
> That thinking holds him to a position that would tend to oppose on principle any kind of overt command-economy thinking, especially when it runs interference with what he would believe, as a fiscally conservative economist, to be a healthy run of market forces. Government interference with the markets, in this view, leads to a worsening of the conditions of hardship caused by such things as inflation and

depression, repression and poverty.

Conversely, Harper would argue against those who see market freedom as a dark thing, requiring regimentation of a powerful state.

That kind of market economy thinking, held on a principled basis, would give any fiscally conservative political leader reason to oppose the Liberal-NDP budget pact and to tremble on the edge of ambiguity with respect to the Goodale budget which preceded it.

* * *

My point will become more obvious when I briefly retell the story of Walter Block. Retell, I say, because, since when I first met Block, in the early '80s, I have found occasion, from time to time, to reintroduce my readers of the moment to him.

At the time I first encountered Block, he was director of the Centre for Religion and Economics (CRE) of the Fraser Institute, the Vancouver-based economically conservative think-tank.

Block told me, at the time, about how he first came to propose the idea of a body that could research the relationship between religion and economics from a market-oriented viewpoint. It happened after he returned from the synagogue, one Sabbath, having heard his rabbi suggest for the umpteenth time that faith-based social justice required the subjugation of market forces and the acceptance of a Marxist-based understanding of economics.

Block spent the next few years working with a whole range of academics and leaders in religious groups to acquaint them with the idea of giving free rein to a market economy. He advocated that such thinking needed the undergirding of a compassionate religious and ethical subculture, because the markets, in and of themselves, could at times be hostile.

Block's chief contribution to the thinking of that period was the organizing, in August 1982, of an international symposium by the CRE. The subject of the symposium, held in Vancouver, was Morality of the Market: Religious and Economic Perspectives.

The event drew together a number of the best minds in the field, from a range of religious, political, and economic viewpoints. Probably the best known, at the time, was Michael Novak of the American Enterprise Institute. His seminal work, *The Spirit of Democratic Capitalism*, created among many religious people the idea that faith was not incompatible with capitalism.

In 1991, after twelve years at the Fraser Institute, Block let it be known that he wanted to research and teach in a religious academic setting, believing that academe could benefit from a disavowal of the resident intelligence that God is on the side of Marxian analysis.

While remaining devoutly Jewish, he recognized that his best teaching opportunity might be in a Christian university.

So, in 1991, he became an associate professor of economics at Holy Cross College in Worcester, Massachusetts, where he stayed until 1997.

After a stint at the University of Central Arkansas,

he moved, in 2001, to Loyola University, New Orleans, a Jesuit institution, where he holds the title Harold E. Wirth Eminent Scholar Chair in Economics and Professor of Economics.

All of which is to say that faith-based fiscal conservatives, if they wish, can find the same academic and cultural support for their positions as do their brothers and sisters in the social conservative world. It is a good deal more cerebral and less emotive than some of the efforts to advocate for traditional family and life viewpoints.

But this kind of support is just as significant in the interplay of faith and politics as is social advocacy.

The Block story indicates, if nothing else, how the informing role that faith often plays in the life of devout politicians finds its personification in Stephen Harper, in his opposition strategy as it relates to what Conservatives have come to describe as the Liberal-NDP budget.

Having noted that, let's touch on the late-May flurry about Christian candidates with a "hidden agenda." The *Globe and Mail* gave legs to the story for several days as its reporters played up the successful nominations of eight Christian Conservative candidates, three in British Columbia, two in Ontario, and three in Atlantic Canada. The point of the stories was that social conservative advocacy groups were so tightly tied to the Conservatives that they were dominating nomination races to help anti-abortion, anti-gay marriage Christians get into Parliament. The potential for conflict, from a media standpoint, was obvious. It was not too hard to uncover battles between socon and procon (Red Tory former Progressive Conservatives) in which the aim was to kill each other off before the "other side" could damage the party too much.

The groups named as those allegedly holding the nomination reins were Defend Marriage, headed by Charles McVety of charismatic-leaning Canada Christian College, and Equipping Christians for the Marketplace, run by Tristan Emmanuel, an orthodox Presbyterian minister. According to the *Globe and Mail*, Emmanuel had helped to engineer the nominations of three Atlantic Conservative candidates. Additionally, Rondo Thomas, a vice-president at McVety's college, had taken the Tory nomination in Ajax-Pickering, just east of Toronto.

A different set of organizations was linked with the other four nominations. David Sweet, running in Ancaster-Dundas-Flamborough-Westdale, was identified as a former president of PromiseKeepers Canada, an evangelical men's organization. Darrel Reid, running in Richmond, B.C., was the former president of Focus on the Family Canada. Cindy Silver, the Tory candidate in North Vancouver, formerly worked for the Christian Legal Fellowship, an organization to which John Weston, running in West Vancouver–Sunshine Coast–Sea to Sky Country, is also linked.

Unclear in the stories was whether these candidates were beholden to the organizations to which they were linked. In other words, were they single-issue candidates committed to press their backers' agendas in a Conservative caucus?

A close examination of the Defend Marriage and Equipping Christians organizations shows considerably more potential for candidates they back being single issue than those with links to PromiseKeepers, Christian Legal

Fellowship, and Focus on the Family. The latter three, after all, have informed the candidates' political views but have not been involved in helping to secure their nominations. Defend Marriage and Equipping Christians seem to have been more directly involved in advising or even helping potential nominees to sell memberships.

Interestingly, as the *Globe and Mail* wound down with the story, it ran an editorial on May 30, 2005, in which it opened with the statement that "it is difficult to understand the fuss about Christian activists helping to secure the nominations of at least eight federal Conservative candidates in the next election." Allowing that the newspaper has argued strongly in favour of same-sex marriage, the editorial pointed out that "the candidates . . . engaging the democratic process to make their arguments is all to the good." It continued,

> How much traction the evangelically supported candidates will have in the broader political arena will depend on how, as individuals, they meld their faith with their role as prospective servants of the people. . . .
>
> The Conservatives know how damaging an allegation of harbouring a "hidden agenda" can be. But there is no innate contradiction between being staunchly religious and politically involved. Democracy invites all comers, and leaves the public to decide who's right for the job.

In effect, the *Globe and Mail* was agreeing with Stephen Harper and, before him, Preston Manning and Brian Mulroney with respect to the way party leaders should

handle people of faith who want to be involved in the political process. And, ultimately, Harper will stand or fall, more
than anything, on his ability to keep the five or six different
kinds of conservatives working together. He has all kinds in
his shadow cabinet.

So what does this all mean for Harper's continuing pilgrimage? Harper does not know, at this point, when he and
Paul Martin will face off in the next federal election.
Strategist that he is reputed to be, it makes sense that he will
feature his shadow cabinet members in their various roles,
allowing them to articulate the platform that the new party
wants to take into the next election.

If Harper does that, by pressing amendments that might
get through the Commons in a minority situation, measures
that would fail if the Liberals had a majority government, he
could well go to the electorate with a two-edged sword. His
party, more than the aging Liberals, has the potential to
communicate both a clean and a competent image — and
the hope that after an election that image could quickly
become reality.

We have learned much about Harper since he first entered
elective politics in 1993, yet we have much still to learn.
While there has been a fair amount of ink spilled about him
in daily journalism, what you have just read is only the
second book about him. William Johnson's *Stephen Harper
and the Future of Canada* was published in June 2005.

Neither Johnson nor I was granted an interview with
Harper during our researching and writing. From my perspective, I am not unhappy about that. The role of a
political journalist is sometimes to be face to face with the
subject politician and sometimes to remain a close observer.

For me, the latter was much the better opportunity than the former.

And it could be argued, too, that Harper did not want to place either himself or his biographers in conflict. He is certainly aware, from his reflections on both Preston Manning and Brian Mulroney, that an arm's-length relationship with journalists or political compatriots is, more often than not, a safe distance.

Certainly, Manning pointed out to me during his comments about Harper, as a political leader widens his or her base, contacts with those who might have been considered close confidants earlier become more tenuous. The result sometimes is that resentment can build up in people who believe their viewpoints are being ignored.

But the fact is that both the grounding and the broadening that Harper has experienced in the years of his pilgrimage will play out critically as he works toward the next election. And the progress of his story will be determined not only by his politics but also by his faith, his family, and his comfort with both what he has shaped and what has shaped him.

However it turns out, the Stephen Harper pilgrimage will bear close examination to determine whether the path he has walked so far will lead him home to the leadership to which he seems, ever less reluctantly, to aspire.

CHAPTER TWELVE

The New Prime Minister

Six weeks after the Conservative Party was elected to minority government status, the first interview with Prime Minister Stephen Harper appeared in *Maclean's*, on March 6, 2006. Asking the questions was Linda Frum, daughter of the late CBC journalistic icon Barbara Frum and sister to David, a noted conservative columnist and senior researcher for the conservative-minded Washington think-tank the American Enterprise Institute. The last question that Frum asked produced a somewhat surprising answer from the PM.

"Why do you think the most popular Liberals have decided not to run for leader?" she inquired of Harper.

After replying that he would not answer the question, he

noted that, in his quest to "put together the strongest government I can assemble," he would be "working not just on the base that we have, but particularly bringing in people from the Liberal party and others, who we believe can support us in the future."

A close examination of Harper's pre-prime ministerial experience would bear out his commitment not only to enlarging the Conservative tent but also looking around corners to see where conservative voters and politicians had been lurking since the election of the Jean Chrétien Liberals thirteen years before. Harper knew full well that many of those in the east had drained into the separatist Bloc Québécois, following the lead of Lucien Bouchard, who had bolted in 1990 from the Mulroney cabinet. Harper could also see many of them in the former Canadian Alliance in western Canada. These were people who, like himself, had been Progressive Conservative voters and workers during the Mulroney era and had moved into the Reform Party, which he himself had played a major role in starting. But there were many others, particularly in Canada's two largest English-speaking cities, Toronto and Vancouver, who were loath to duck out from under the Liberal banner.

How to break the log jam? That was Harper's main challenge in his quest for majority government in the next election after 2006. His answer to that challenge was to persuade David Emerson, the industry minister in Paul Martin's Liberal cabinet, to switch to the Conservative Party and become international trade minister in his own new cabinet.

There were a couple of good reasons for that gambit. Emerson represented Vancouver Kingsway, an eclectic urban riding representative of those city enclaves that might not be ready for political realignment just yet. In addition, he was not a partisan Liberal and, in fact, had surprised many on the West Coast who knew him by accepting Martin's invitation to be a "star candidate" in the 2004 election. Before entering elective politics, Emerson was a deputy minister serving under the Social Credit regime in British Columbia. Later he became president of CanFor, which dominated the forest industry in the province. It was in those capacities that John Reynolds, the now-retired West Vancouver MP and campaign co-chair for the 2006 election, had come to know Emerson years before.

British Columbia is one of three provinces whose centre-right political sectors are presided over by one party rather than two. It has been that way on the West Coast since the early 1940s, when a Liberal-Conservative coalition ruled under Byron (Boss) Johnson. When that cluster broke up, W.A.C. Bennett and, later, his son, Bill Bennett, reigned under the Social Credit banner for a cumulative thirty-two years. And, when Social Credit died, the B.C. Liberals, a Liberal-Tory amalgam, formed and virtually swept the province in 2001. They were re-elected by a smaller but still comfortable margin in 2005. (The other two provinces with right-centre fusions, rather than two distinct parties splitting that support, are Saskatchewan and Quebec. But that is fodder for another story or two.)

Reynolds knew Emerson well enough to figure that he would not necessarily remain under the Liberal banner. But he could not easily make his move until after the Tories came to power. That there was a move to be made was the subject of an interesting premonition, which I recounted in an Ottawa *Watch* column that I wrote on February 14, 2006.

Less than a decade ago, the United Alternative movement was developing in an effort to morph the Reform Party into something that might help reunite the Conservative movement. At that time, the venerable and sometimes mischievous Peter C. Newman had a suggestion for the leader of whatever came out of the UA talks.

Newman's suggestion was one Paul Martin. His rationale, as I recall, was that Jean Chrétien was going to do all he could to block Martin's ascension to the Liberal leadership. He indicated that, as finance minister, Martin had shown himself to be vaguely similar to a fiscal conservative, so a jump to lead a centre-right party might not be as impossible as it seemed.

* * *

That never happened, of course. But its consideration leads to a look at the Conservative Council website (conservativecouncil.ca).

The Conservative Council is a body that attempts to provide a voice to the "left" side of the conservative movement. Its chair, Rick Peterson of Vancouver, would admit that the people for whom he speaks used to be known as Red Tories.

On February 9, Peterson posted an article to the site, entitled "A Global Moment with David Emerson." In that piece, he provided a link to another article he wrote, shortly after the June 2004 election. Its headline read "David Emerson: The First Liberal Defection?"

Peterson's more recent post suggested that "We thought [after the 2004 election] that given Emerson's background in business, he would be more comfortable sitting as a Tory instead of inside the Paul Martin cabinet. Well, it turns out we were right — but just a little early."

In his post-2004 election note, Peterson concluded by pointing out that

> Conservatives working on the [2004] campaign in Vancouver Kingsway . . . say that Emerson let a number of them know that he found it tough to be out campaigning as a Liberal. Keep in mind that he was approached by Paul Martin to run long before the PC-CA merger created the Conservative Party of Canada.

So the Emerson floor-crossing — and its reasons — were identified by Peterson long before they happened.

* * *

Now, post-January 23, 2006, Paul Martin was gone as prime minister.

But before he went, he met with Stephen Harper and, according to his own testimony, had a "good talk," mostly about "international relations."

Martin's departure was pretty classy. And he felt no need to further castigate his successor.

Without being a fly on the wall, there is no way to know if Martin and Harper discussed Emerson and his future. But the fact is that they both knew that Emerson no longer owed any loyalty to the man who had recruited him.

And Harper and his advisors knew, as well, that if Emerson could continue to serve on international files, including the softwood lumber dispute, his value to the new government could be ensured.

* * *

But what about the floor-crossing issue?

There are indications in some quarters at least that Emerson is only the first of at least a dozen to follow.

Now that contention may simply be Conservative wishful thinking. That is only true, however, if it is seen in splendid isolation rather than in the context of a massive multiyear political realignment now seemingly underway.

Paul Jackson, associate editor of the *Calgary Sun,* outlined that context in a piece he wrote Sunday, February 12, 2006, entitled "Bright Outlook: Political Climate Points toward a Decade of Decent Government."

Jackson maintains that there are rumours that "10 or 12 Liberal MPs on the party's right may follow . . . Emerson, cross the floor and join Prime Minister Stephen Harper's Conservatives when parliament opens."

If there is any firm basis for Jackson's suggestion, then Emerson's move is not an isolated happening.

The political realignment, indeed, occurs on three levels. The first took place with the CA-PC merger, when Keith Martin, Scott Brison, and Belinda Stronach moved to the Liberals.

The move to the Conservatives was much less pronounced.

First John Bryden walked the floor but failed to win the 2004 Ancaster-Dundas-Flamborough-Westdale Tory nomination. That was taken by David Sweet, who lost to the Liberals in 2004 but won on in 2006.

Then David Kilgour, the veteran Edmonton MP who had sat for equal time since 1979 for the Conservatives and the Liberals, became an independent and promptly quit politics to do foreign aid work. He did not join the Tories but did give support to several Conservative candidates in this year's election.

So that is the first level.

The second is the reparking of conservative voters from the Liberals to the Tories. That has taken place, especially in Ontario, in the last two elections, when the Conservatives jumped from two seats in 2000 to over 20 in 2004 and 40 in 2006.

The third level will be the moving of long-time social and/or fiscal conservative Liberal MPs to the Tories.

That is a much tougher proposition, given that it means moving from a familiar political culture, where they have been at home for years, into a new setting. There they may have to compete with old-time Reformers and Progressive Conservatives for place and influence.

But Harper is incrementally gaining experience in this process.

After all, he has effected the PC-CA merger when many suggested it would fail. And, in so doing, he has won kudos from both Brian Mulroney and Preston Manning.

And he has done something else, which went almost unnoticed in the Emerson furor.

He has both Chuck Strahl and Stockwell Day in the same cabinet.

The two men were on opposite sides of the fence when Day's leadership of the Canadian Alliance was called into question. Strahl led the dissident group that actually left the

Alliance caucus at that time and teamed up in a parliamentary coalition then led by Progressive Conservative leader Joe Clark. (The dissidents returned to the Alliance after Harper became CA leader, bringing with them the results of careful cultivation with then PC deputy leader Peter MacKay — relations that would serve the two parties well when the CA-PC merger process took place.)

Sometimes it takes a while. Wounds need healing. Realities need recognizing. But both men are now positioned to do work for which they have well prepared themselves: Day as public safety minister and Strahl in the agriculture portfolio.

In biblical terms, we sometimes refer to Harper's task as "lengthening the cords and strengthening the stakes." And indicators are that, while the wind may whistle around the edges at times, the tent is widening nicely.

So, strategically speaking, Harper's move to bring in Emerson was a prelude to attracting other urban Liberal MPs into the Conservative caucus. Will it actually happen? As of mid-2006, it has not. Rather, one hears the occasional suggestion, from Liberal insiders, that many of the more conservatively acceptable Liberals will retire from politics. In so doing, they will quietly leave their ridings open to new, strong, and well-fitted Conservative candidates: sort of a renewal by attrition. All that would help to position Harper to make Tory breakthroughs in Vancouver and Toronto in the next election as well as in many of the rural and small-city ridings still held by Liberals, in areas of Ontario outside Toronto.

In many ways, the Liberals seemed to be cooperating with that political realignment concept as they worked their way toward electing a replacement for Paul Martin. There was a definite leftward tilt toward the leadership campaign, egged on by the three front-runners, Michael Ignatieff, Bob Rae (the former NDP premier of Ontario), and Stéphane Dion. That tilt was to be expected, especially after Canadian Autoworkers Union head Buzz Hargrove urged his members to vote strategically to re-elect the Liberals and keep the Tories out in the 2006 election. He did so in obvious contradiction to NDP leader Jack Layton, in whose party he was considerably influential: Layton spent the election attacking the Liberals and maintaining that he could work with the Conservatives. Harper, for his part, spoke frequently of collaborating with the NDP should he form a minority government. *Walrus* magazine, in fact, picked up on that theme in its May 2006 issue, with a major essay by NDP insider James Laxer, entitled "Fake Left, Go Right." The cover blurb for the article read "Neo-Conned: How the NDP Fell for Stephen Harper." For his efforts, Hargrove got a bear hug from Paul Martin during the 2006 campaign, at a Liberal gathering in Ontario's autoworker heartland, and the revoking of his longtime membership in the Ontario NDP, shortly after the January vote.

From where he was sitting, Harper could take courage from all this. As long as he remained anchored in the principles embodied by the several branches of conservatism that made up the Conservative Party, and continued to reach out to conservative-thinking people who had been voting Liberal and NDP for the previous two decades, he could benefit from the left-leaning efforts of the Liberals. Indeed, the Tories could survive any Liberal-NDP merger or cooperation that might come out of a leftward rejigging, as long as they got their dibs in first.

As Harper increasingly planted his prime ministerial feet firmly under his desk, he showed every indication that he was more comfortable in his new role than he was as opposition leader. Sue Riley, a left-leaning *Ottawa Citizen/CanWest* columnist, offered a couple of reasons that emanated from the care with which Harper had been building his leadership skills and positioning during his time in opposition. On March 24, in an *Ottawa Citizen* column entitled "The Luck of the Clever," Riley noted that Harper "measures every word, and, while no politician is bulletproof, this one will be hard to catch in a contradiction." Earlier in the piece, she observed that "Harper resolved to do things differently and, so far, he has. In fact, for so emotionally contained a leader, he has displayed surprising sensitivity to the traumas, and triumphs, of ordinary people caught in extraordinary circumstances." Her point, in part, was that, while Harper was new to the prime minister's role, "he does have a thick portfolio of speeches as opposition leader." Often such speeches are capable of derailing an aspiring political leader. But, as noted prior to the election, Harper is skilled at nuancing his words — as well as simplifying his language — to prevent misunderstanding and raised expectations.

Two weeks later, on April 7, Riley wrote, in another *Ottawa Citizen* column, that "Stephen Harper is proving to be a different kind of leader. In public, he can sound inflexible, arrogant and reflexively competitive — he behaves, at times, as if he won a crushing majority in January. But, behind the scenes, he is showing surprising flexibility and a talent for intelligent compromise."

Riley used the child-care program to illustrate her point.

She argued that child care is ideologically loaded for the Conservatives, "who portray their $1,200 annual baby bonus as putting parents ahead of 'experts, bureaucrats and interest groups.' But," she continued,

> there may be room for negotiation on the other half of the Tory plan: $250 million in tax credits to employers and community groups to create 125,000 new spaces over five years.
>
> This scheme (which didn't work when Mike Harris tried it) is meant to replace deals the Liberals signed with the provinces to create a national child-care network. Some saw hope, in the vague language of the throne speech, that Tory "incentives" may be broad enough to include grants for non-profit groups and even money for provinces. This could mollify premiers and middle-class parents who need child-care spaces, not cash.

In noting that the Mike Harris plan apparently did not work, Riley picked up on the main argument that Liberal leadership hopefuls had been offering during their campaigns to devalue the Tory strategy. Implicit in the criticism was that conservative social policy, relying on non-state initiative, is bound to fail.

And that is the challenge for Harper.

He will want to demonstrate the long-established, western-based, populist definition of social conservatism. While it includes traditional life and family matters, it broadens to take into account issues raised from a socialist or social democratic perspective but works toward solutions that come out of a conservative grounding. That is why child care and, to a lesser extent, the environment are real tests for that resolve.

Riley rightly pointed out that Harper has committed to 125,000 child-care spaces. And he has done so in the face of statistics on both sides of the issue. Social conservatives say that the demand for professional, non-family child care is simply not there — at least not nearly to the extent that universal daycare advocates claim it to be. And those advocates, burdened as they are with the conviction that professional child care is often superior to that provided by parents and relatives, have long worked at building the case for a state-controlled system.

For now, Harper has established a climate for public consideration of a fiscally and socially conservative child-care policy by introducing the $1,200 annual child-care payment to parents for every child under six. And he has promised an allocation of $250 million in next year's budget for various kinds of child-care spaces. He — or, more specifically, his human resources development minister, Diane Finley — speaks of creating options such as tax credits for corporations that want to operate at-work, not-for-profit child-care centres and grants for non-profit and other "boutique"-type facilities. And in so doing, Harper fires a shot across the bow of the early childhood education advocates' ship. He says, in effect, that the Liberals never really created spaces, that nobody on the federal level has ever tried to build a strong system on a fiscally and socially conservative model. What the Liberals did, in the Harper scenario, is promise the provinces money for a system that would tend to cut out parents and cut in professionals without having thought their way through the whole process.

Kyoto presents a similar challenge. Harper needs to present a conservative solution to replace a liberal one that appears to have some serious flaws. In bringing forward these various conservative scenarios, Harper is looking at both the Brian Mulroney record, two decades ago, and the ongoing informal guidance system centred on some of the thinking of his former mentor, Preston Manning. The Mulroney "green" record fortuitously came to Harper's aid in late spring 2006, when several environmental groups decided to honour his Tory predecessor for being the "greenest prime minister ever." The green coalition threw a party for Mulroney at Ottawa's Fairmont Château Laurier, emceed by his television host son Ben. And they asked none other than Stephen Harper to introduce him to the gathered assemblage.

In lauding Mulroney, many of the speakers suggested that sometimes it is difficult for non-conservative environmentalists to admit to themselves that it is possible to be both green and conservative. And, in so doing, they created, perhaps inadvertently, a platform that would allow Harper and his environment minister, Rona Ambrose, to strike out a new, conservative course that would surprise even the most left-leaning environmentalist with its effectiveness. In introducing Mulroney, Harper suggested that the chance for such an occasion to take place ten years ago — one in which the former prime minister was being feted by a former deputy of the Reform Party — would have been unbelievable.

Which brings us to Preston Manning.

Harper's success to date relates, in part at least, to his willingness to accept the counsel of both Mulroney and Manning. Harper does this in different ways. With

Mulroney, he asks for advice and listens — literally. After all, the former prime minister is not saying much for the record these days, so Harper cannot read up on his latest views or suggestions based on past experience. And Harper relied heavily on key people from the Mulroney era during the transition into government.

Manning, however, has evolved into a "senior statesperson" with a think-tank to boot. His considered prognostications are regularly published in the *Globe and Mail,* and his Manning Centre for Building Democracy is seen as a significant conservative base able to provide political leaders with some of the communication, research, and educational counsel they might need. Because some of his work is published, it means that Harper can read Manning's thinking without picking up the phone or sending an e-mail. And he has the benefit of knowing, while he is reading the latest Manning piece, that at least 100,000 or so other Canadians are doing so as well, among them a fair number of community or national leaders.

On June 28, 2006, Manning's article in the *Globe and Mail* had a fair amount of specific advice for Harper and Ambrose concerning Kyoto and the Tory promise to replace it with a "made-in-Canada" plan. In a humorous vein, Manning answered the question by noting that, "as a general rule, Canadians prefer to avoid either/or decisions altogether. We are tempted to follow the advice of that great American philosopher Yogi Berra, who said: 'When you come to a fork in the road, take it.'" Manning continued:

> A wiser course would be to heed the advice of British author C. S. Lewis. Mr. Lewis observed that in

the real world, we simply cannot avoid "either/or" situations. . . .

[Lewis said that] we live in a world where every road, after a few miles, forks into two, and each of those into two again. At each fork, we must make a decision. We cannot pursue both roads simultaneously, and if it becomes apparent that we have chosen the wrong road, we should not continue to go down it, expecting that some adjustment or future development will somehow turn it into the right road. Having chosen the wrong road, said Mr. Lewis, there is only one corrective action possible, and that is to go back to the fork where the error was made and proceed from there in a different direction.

He concluded with this encouragement to the prime minister:

The remedy is not, as the Harper government has realized, to continue down the same road, hoping the passage of time or some revised federal commitment to an unworkable agreement will somehow produce a better result. The remedy is to go back to the fork in the road where the error was first made — to the point where the federal government decided to proceed unilaterally, rather than in partnership with the provinces and private sector, to address the environmental consequences of hydrocarbon combustion — and proceed from there to hammer out a new and better co-operative approach.

This is my understanding of the road the new

environment minister is endeavouring to map out and follow. The first step is to get back to that pivotal fork in the road.

Partisan though it may seem to be at first glance, Manning's advice seems to be to go back beyond the fork in the road that Jean Chrétien took to the path that the "greenest" PM was taking — in that context — in the 1980s and early 1990s.

Before wrapping up this post-election view of the new prime minister, let's tackle the question of how he has handled the faith-based social conservatives. The most ardent of them point out clearly that he is not one of them. He is ambiguous on abortion and has no problem with same-sex "civil unions," even though he is committed to the traditional definition of marriage. But they admit that he is better than the Liberal alternative.

Reporting for Canadian Catholic News and the *Catholic Register,* Parliament Hill journalist Deborah Gyapong suggested that the cabinet composition is widely considered good news, with one-third of the new ministers being pro-life and pro-marriage. Gyapong quoted Campaign Life Coalition, a major pro-life and pro-traditional marriage group, as identifying nine pro-life, pro-marriage ministers. They are (with portfolios in parentheses) Jim Flaherty (finance), Chuck Strahl (agriculture), Vic Toews (justice), Loyola Hearn (fisheries), Monte Solberg (citizenship and immigration), Rob Nicholson (democratic reform), Stockwell Day (public safety), Gary Lunn (natural resources), and Carol Skelton (national revenue). And she quoted yours truly accurately in noting that "veteran journalist Lloyd Mackey [said] the social conservatives in cabinet are known for being 'incremental' in their approach to social change. Mackey said they are less likely to lobby for legislative changes such as banning abortions but to seek more 'indirect means' to reduce the number of abortions, for example."

To that I would add that there are both pro-life and pro-choice people in the cabinet. With Harper's incremental approach, the people in the two camps are expected to respect each other and, for that matter, the Constitution. That means socons will try to encourage a reduction in the number of abortions, with full respect for the views of their colleagues who insist on a woman's right to choose.

And, of course, as public policy issues move forward, no matter who is in power, pro-lifers will increasingly focus on euthanasia. Gyapong quoted Euthanasia Prevention Coalition executive director Alex Schadenberg as suggesting that he was "thankful" Vic Toews is in the justice post. He pointed to Toews's work as opposition justice critic, in managing the Conservatives' handling of the marriage debate, and his personal opposition to the Bloc-initiated assisted suicide proposal, known as Bill C-407.

In finalizing this analysis of the new Harper government, I could have drawn on any number of pundits who were generally pleasantly surprised at how well the first six months had gone for the Conservatives. The one I chose was John Redekop, who was, for many years, head of the Department of Political Science at Wilfrid Laurier University and remains a professor emeritus there. He is retired in British Columbia, where he is an adjunct political science prof at Trinity Western University. Redekop is not only a political science specialist but also an ordained evangelical minister, of Mennonite persuasion. That makes him, in my view, a useful analyst in seeing how Harper has done in integrating the various kinds of conservatism, including those with a faith base. In a "report card" piece published in the July 3, 2006, issue of the *Kitchener-Waterloo Record,* Redekop gave the Harper Conservatives an A- overall, with a range from B- to A+ in thirteen areas of activity. I will include a quotation from Redekop for each of the areas, including some where he is fairly critical, as a preface to my wrap on this examination of Prime Minister Stephen Harper's political and governmental focus.

Cabinet development and performance: B. "Well balanced in all important respects . . . generally competent, focused and well-disciplined." Redekop was critical of the David Emerson and Michael Fortier appointments, however, saying that, while they were defensible, they were, in Emerson's case, too quick and, in Fortier's, contradictory to his previous stances.

Performance in the House of Commons: A. The Conservatives did "amazingly well . . . clearly outperforming the official opposition. All opposition parties revealed their relative ineffectiveness when they voted unanimously for the Conservative's $187 billion budget without realizing it."

Social policies: B+. "The main weakness [in the child-care grant] is that a single mother working for a living will keep much less than a mother who stays at home while her husband earns $100,000 a year." While the Conservative rejection of the $5.1 billion Kelowna Accord was not explained well, "their quick provision of clean water for aboriginals and their $450 million housing initiative indicated acceptance of at least some accord goals."

Economic policies: B+. While widely welcomed, the weakness in the one percent reduction in the GST is that "there is no way of ensuring that the reduction will not be passed on in those situations where the tax is built into the selling price. The budget included 29 tax reductions which, in total, brought more tax relief than the previous four budgets combined."

Foreign affairs: B. While the Conservatives deserve credit for bringing a softwood lumber pact "much closer" than the Liberals had, "it is, in fact, far from being a done deal." While the prime minister's trip to Afghanistan was a "great success," the Harper government "may yet find that trying to bring order and democracy to Muslim Afghanistan is much less likely to be successful than has been assumed."

National unity policies: A-. "Marked success: The more enlightened and conciliatory attitude toward Quebec has resulted in declining support for sovereignty." That said, "the recent backtracking [on the fiscal imbalance], especially by Finance Minister Jim Flaherty, has disappointed many Quebecers and antagonized virtually all provincial governments."

Environmental policies: B. "The Liberal commitment was meaningless, a miserable and total failure. The Conservatives are, however, vulnerable because they are taking a long time to develop their alternate program. Only time will tell whether a truly worthwhile set of proposals will be forthcoming."

Crime and justice policies: A+. "Killing the long-gun registry was long overdue. . . . Registering gun owners [the new Conservative policy] makes more sense. The legislation against street-racing, the introduction of tougher minimum sentences, the arming of border guards and the expansion of the RCMP by 1,000 members all make a lot of sense. While the $26 million for victims and the $20 million for crime prevention are rather modest sums, they constitute important steps."

Defence and military policies: A+. "This peacekeeping country had hardly any people or equipment with which to keep the peace! At last the country has a government which understands what defence procurement means and is willing to adopt responsible policies." (As a Mennonite clergyman, Redekop tends to encourage peacemaking and downplay the military's combat role. That should be taken into account in his giving the government such a high grade in the defence category.)

Parliamentary reform: A. "The Federal Accountability Act, if passed by the Senate without significant revision, will mark the greatest step forward in this area that the country has ever seen. The eight-year term for senators is a significant reform as is the appointment of senators who have been previously elected in their provinces."

Specific initiatives: B. Redekop commends several "secondary . . . and necessary" policy initiatives, including cancelling the "give away" sale of the Prince Rupert Coal Terminal, the reviewing of Supreme Court appointments, the proposal for a Public Appointments Commission, the unequivocal apology to Chinese Canadians for the head tax, the listing of the Tamil Tigers as a banned terrorist organization, and the termination of having half-mast flags at the Peace Tower for deceased soldiers. More questionable — even lamentable — have been the tensions between Harper and the parliamentary press gallery.

Keeping election promises: A. "The Harper team has done

very well in this area. . . . Where the Paul Martin regime largely dithered, [they] mostly acted, perhaps even a bit hastily. . . . [T]he overall record . . . is impressive."

The overall leadership of Prime Minister Harper: A. "Much more impressive as prime minister than . . . as opposition leader. He has been decisive and focused. He has made some errors . . . but, by and large, he has handled himself with dignity, aplomb and even with distinction."

In listening to some within Harper's various circles — inner, middle, outer — the prime minister's sure-footedness has been evident, even as the critics begin grinding potentially controversial Middle East statements. On July 14, 2006, while travelling to his first G8 Summit in St. Petersburg, Russia, Harper made the point that Hezbollah, not Israel, was the aggressor in the Lebanese flare-up and that Israel was right to defend itself. This was a rather blunt departure from contemporary Liberal thinking that tended to leave the general populace with the impression that Hezbollah was some sort of service agency committed simply to winning for the Lebanese Muslims what had long been a given for their old archrivals, the Israelis.

Interestingly, the strongest support for Harper came from John Manley, Liberal foreign affairs minister during the latter part of Jean Chrétien's tenure. Manley wrote an article published in the July 28, 2006, *Ottawa Citizen*. Background to Harper's position is that both Manley and Harper, contrasting as they may be in their viewpoints in their political philosophy, have access to those groups of Canadians who strongly articulate cultural, religious, and philosophical viewpoints in defence of a permanent place for Israel in the Middle East scheme of things. That Harper could speak as he did is a clear sign that he may not be too far off base in his first Middle East pronouncement. But there are other shoes to drop.

* * *

Reviewing all that I wrote about Stephen Harper prior to the 2006 election, in which I tried to describe both his political and his spiritual pilgrimage (and that of the party that he brought together from five or six different strands), I would agree with much of what Redekop and Manley had to say. In the areas of faith and family, he has remained true to his moorings, without trying to lay his own trip on anyone else. In bringing conservative policies and principles into the larger political arena, he has generally acted wisely and incrementally. He wants to make sure that what is proposed will work to the greater good.

Harper continues to exhibit an engagingly stubborn streak. Don't be surprised if the "give chase approach" that brought Peter MacKay and the Progressive Conservatives to the merger table serves equally well in finally getting the softwood lumber dispute settled.

People who suggest that Harper is intolerant or dismissive of the views of others misunderstand, I believe, his approach to information gathering. My experience has been that he challenges those who bring their views or concerns to him to deliver their arguments in a cogent and orderly manner and thereby convince him. Harper is very bright, and he uses his intelligence to work through all the information with which he is presented so that, when he communicates with his compatriots and his public, his message is brief and clear.

When I agreed, shortly after the 2004 election, to write this book, there was great uncertainty about how long Harper would be around. He was devastated by the loss to the Liberals and thought long and hard about whether he would continue in political life. At the time, I expressed the view that he had come too far to quit then.

Winning a minority government in 2006 has not disappointed Harper but made him more determined to win a majority as soon as it is reasonably possible. And *reasonably* is the operative word.

If Harper can make a collaborative Parliament work in a minority situation, then he will not press too hard to make the opposition bring him down. Having set in place the idea of a fixed election date in 2009, he may well have triggered a parliamentary mood that will be more inclined to encourage principled collaboration.

So the pilgrimage of Stephen Harper could still have a few years to run. And if he keeps his eye on the ball, his legacy could turn out to be a "best practices" example of the Canadian penchant for peace, order, and good government.

Index

Block, Walter, 207, 210
Bloedow, Jonathan, 47, 48
B'nai B'rith, 92
Boessenkool, Ken, 72–73, 156–61,
    165, 170–71
Boessenkool, Tammy, 72, 156
Bouchard, Lucien, 216
Bracken, John, 16, 54
Breitkreuz, Garry, 106–9
Brimelow, Peter, 154
Brison, Scott, 220
British Toryism, 54
Broadbent, Ed, 114
Bryden, John, 220
Burke, Edmund, 101, 138, 169
Byfield, Ted, 123, 137–38, 145, 169

Calgary Centre-North, 31
Calgary Herald, 27, 55, 153
Calgary Prophetic Bible Institute,
    84
"Calgary School," 58, 72, 111, 119,
    134, 141–45, 165, 186
Calgary Southwest, 94–95
Calgary Sun, 220
Calgary West, xix, 1, 18, 25–26, 29
Calgary–Nose Hill, 60, 182
Campaign Life Canada, 103, 230
Campbell, Douglas, 17
Campbell, Gordon, 203
Canada Christian College, 113, 211
Canada Health Act, 128–32, 172
Canada Pension Plan, 172
Canada West Foundation, 39, 123
Canadian Alliance, 4–6, 14, 46,
    58, 82, 90–91, 94, 103, 105–6,
    111–12, 137–38, 142, 158–59,

161–64, 179, 186, 189, 197, 216,
    221-22
Canadian Autoworkers Union,
    223
Canadian Broadcasting
    Corporation (cbc), 41, 122, 155
Canadian Catholic News, 230
Canadian Club, Ottawa, 173
Canadian Constitution, The, 231
Canadian Parliamentary Press
    Gallery, xiii, 23, 104, 115–17,
    146, 178
Canadian Reformed Church, 72,
    156
Canadian Wheat Board, 167
CanFor, 217
CanWest Foundation, 224
Caouette, Réal, 86, 100
Carty, Ken, 166, 203–4
Catholic Register, 230
CBC, 215
Centre for Building Canadian
    Democracy, 123, 134
Centre Street Church, Calgary,
    60, 66
CF-18 contract, 45
Charest, Jean, 84, 147, 154, 157
Charismatic Christianity, 65, 69,
    76, 90–91, 156, 201
Charter of Rights and Freedoms,
    152, 166–67
Chesterton, G. K., 74
Chrétien, Jean, 11–12, 38, 48, 60,
    80–81, 150, 154, 171, 174, 216,
    218, 230, 235
Christian and Missionary Alliance
    Church, 26, 47, 65–66, 69

Jackson, Paul, 220
Jaffer, Rahim, 107
Johnson, Byron (Boss), 217
Johnson, Daniel, 154
Johnson, William, xiii, xvii, 60,
  154, 213

Kee, Kevin, 83
Kelowna Accord, The, 232
Kenney, Jason, 104, 115
Keynes, John Maynard, 34–39
Kilgour, David, xi, 9, 60, 80–81,
  113–14, 221
Kim, Victor, 31
King, William Lyon Mackenzie,
  83
Kitchener-Waterloo Record, The,
  232
Klein, Ralph, 123, 165, 171, 180
Knopff, Rainer, 144, 171
Kyoto Accord, 167, 227-28

La Marsh, Judy, 198
Lang, Michelle, 27
Laxer, James, 223
Layton, Jack, 194, 199, 223
LeBreton, Marjory, 106–10
Leclair, Father Joe, 69
Lethbridge Community College,
  29
Levant, Ezra, 144, 150
Lewis, C. S., 49, 59–81, 124, 143,
  228-29
Liberal Party of Canada, 80–81,
  94–100, 125–27, 168–74,
  180–85, 192–201, 203–7, 213,
  215-25

Liberal Progressive Party, 154
Libertarianism, 54, 91, 96, 102,
  109, 138–39, 145–46, 177
Lord of the Rings, The, 78
Lunn, Gary, 230

Macarenko, Gloria, 155
Macdonald, John A., 83
MacDonald, Marci, 144–45
MacKay, Peter, x, 6, 25, 56–58,
  100–4, 109, 118–22, 138–42,
  147, 179–80, 184–89, 195–97,
  222, 236
Mackenzie, Alexander, 83
Mackey, Lloyd, 230-31
Maclean's, 215
Mainse, David, 91
Manley, John, 81, 235, 236
Manning Centre for Building
  Democracy, 228
Manning, Ernest, xv, xviii, 27, 29,
  51–55, 64, 80, 84, 186
Manning, Preston, xv, xvi, xviii,
  xix, 2–3, 10, 13, 19, 28, 40 47,
  55, 57, 63–64, 68, 73, 89–90,
  100, 104, 122, 126, 128, 142, 154,
  162, 164, 166, 173, 175–78, 184,
  212–14, 221, 227-30
Manning, Sandra, 47, 64–65, 68
Mansell, Robert, 2, 10, 19–20, 28
Martin, Keith, 107, 220
Martin, Paul, xx, 7, 18–19, 32–33,
  38, 66–68, 79, 123, 129, 133, 161,
  203, 213, 216-17, 218, 222-23, 235
  and Stephen Harper, 219
Mazankowski, Don, 25, 185
McGill University, 83